FOCUS ON Comprehension

Teacher's Resource
for Starter and Introductory Books

Louis Fidge

Nelson

Thomas Nelson and Sons Ltd
Nelson House
Mayfield Road
Walton-on-Thames
Surrey KT12 5PL

Thomas Nelson is
an International Thomson Company

Text © Louis Fidge 1999
Illustrations © Thomas Nelson and Sons Ltd 1999

First published by Thomas Nelson and Sons Ltd 1999
ISBN 0-17-420324-1
9 8 7 6 5 4 3 2
02 01 00 99

All rights reserved. No part of this publication may be reproduced, copied or transmitted in any form or by any means, electronic or mechanical, including photocopy, recording, or any information storage and retrieval system, without permission in writing from the publisher or under licence from the Copyright Licensing Authority Ltd, 90 Tottenham Court Road, London W1P 9HE.

Private purchasers may make copies of the two record sheets, and 88 copymasters in this book for use within and by the staff and students of the institution only.

This permission to copy does not extend to additional institutions or branches of an institution, who should purchase a separate master copy of the book for their own use.

For copying in any other circumstances prior permission must be obtained in writing from Thomas Nelson and Sons Ltd.

Printed in Croatia

Acknowledgements

The author and publishers thank the following for permission to reproduce copyright materials, as follows: June Crebbin for *My Grannies* from *The Jungle Sale* published by Viking Kestrel 1988; Cassell for *Winter Days* by Gareth Owen in *A Christmas Stocking* compiled by Wes Magee; Orchard Books (a division of Watts Publishing Group) for *Bedtime Lullaby* from *First Rhymes* by Lucy Coats 1994; Methuen Children's Books, an imprint of Egmont Children's Books Ltd for the extract from *Now We are Six* © AA Milne Copyright under the Berne Convention (*Wind on the Hill* and *Us Two*); Scholastic Publications for *Wind* by Jean Kenward.

Please note: We have tried to trace and contact all copyright holders before publication, but this has not always been possible. If notified, we, the publishers, will be pleased to make any amendments or arrangements at the first opportunity.

CONTENTS

Introduction – What is comprehension?	4
Statutory and non-statutory guidance	5
Components of *Focus on Comprehension*	7
Overview of range of texts	8
Using *Focus on Comprehension* in the classroom	9
Class record sheet	10
Individual record sheet	11

STARTER BOOK

Note: each unit is accompanied by 3 copymasters providing 3 levels of comprehension.

Unit 1	Get me out!	12
Unit 2	Sam's Busy Week	16
Unit 3	A Number Rhyme	20
Unit 4	The Puddle in the Park	24
Unit 5	Let's Make a Shaker	28
Unit 6	Miss Polly had a Dolly	32
Unit 7	The Gingerbread Man	36
Unit 8	The Princess and the Pea	40
Unit 9	Hoppers and Jumpers	44
Unit 10	Rhymes from Around the World	48
Unit 11	The Deaf Man and the Blind Man	52
Unit 12	An ABC of People	56
Unit 13	King Rollo and the New Shoes	60
Unit 14	Birds in the Rainforest	64
Unit 15	Wind on the Hill	68
Unit 16	Crow's Problem	72
Unit 17	Row Your Boat	76
Unit 18	My Pet Hamster	80
Unit 19	Ready for Winter	84
Unit 20	Messing About	88
Unit 21	A Visit to the Opticians	92
Unit 22	Things are Puzzling	96

INTRODUCTORY BOOK

Note: each unit has an accompanying photocopy master on the facing page.

Unit 1	Alfie's Feet	100
Unit 2	Mice	102
Unit 3	The Car Ride	104
Unit 4	Nursery Rhymes Old and New	106
Unit 5	Making a Peanut Butter and Jam Sandwich	108
Unit 6	Granny, Granny, Please Comb my Hair	110
Unit 7	Willy and Hugh	112
Unit 8	The Hare and the Tortoise	114
Unit 9	About Books	116
Unit 10	Bedtime	118
Unit 11	Face to Face with a Dragon	120
Unit 12	Contents and Index Pages	122
Unit 13	The Blind Men and the Elephant	124
Unit 14	From a Tadpole to a Frog	126
Unit 15	A Dark, Dark Tale	128
Unit 16	Mr Cosmo the Conjuror	130
Unit 17	Neigh, Cluck, Quack and Tweet	132
Unit 18	Valley Farm	134
Unit 19	Animal Homes	136
Unit 20	Pooh Bear Gets Stuck	138
Unit 21	Our Family Comes from Around the World	140
Unit 22	The Winter Hedgehog	142

WHAT IS COMPREHENSION?

The *Concise Oxford Dictionary* defines comprehension as 'the act or capability of understanding, especially writing or speech'. In the context of school, the ability to gain meaning from the printed word is of paramount importance.

A helpful way of looking at comprehension is to treat it as a range of skills. Thomas Barrett, quoted in *Reading Today and Tomorrow*[1], suggests a taxonomy of comprehension skills. This provides a very useful model, and was used as a framework for developing and structuring the *Focus on Comprehension* series

Barrett divides reading comprehension into five major skill levels which move from the easy to the difficult in terms of the demands they place on the reader. The categories he suggests are:

▶ Literal Comprehension
   This focuses on ideas and information explicitly stated in the text. The tasks may involve recognition or recall of details, main ideas, sequences, cause and effect, character traits and so on.
▶ Reorganisation
   This requires the child to analyse and/or reorganise ideas or information explicitly stated in the text. For example, tasks may involve classifying, outlining or summarising.
▶ Inferential Comprehension
   This requires the child to use information and ideas explicitly stated in the text, along with intuition and personal experiences as a basis for making deductions and hypotheses. The child is required to use thinking and imagination that go beyond the printed page.
▶ Evaluation
   This requires the reader to evaluate a text, by comparing ideas presented with external criteria (such as other similar sources), or internal criteria (such as by drawing on the reader's own experiences, knowledge or values). Evaluative comprehension deals with qualities of accuracy, acceptability, desirability, worth or probability of occurrence.
▶ Appreciation
   This involves the subjective response of the impact of the text on the reader. It requires some sort of emotional response to the content, characters or incidents, author's use of language or imagery.

In summary, categories of Barrett's taxonomy of comprehension skills are as follows:
▶ read the lines (using literal comprehension)
▶ read between the lines (using reorganisation and inference)
▶ read beyond the lines (using evaluative and appreciative comprehension).

Focus on Comprehension used this three-fold classification to develop three categories of differentiated activities, designed to help children develop a wide range of comprehension skills.

---

[1] T. Barrett, quoted in Theodore Clymer, 'What is reading? Some current concepts', Open University 1968 in *Reading Today and Tomorrow*, University of London Press 1972.

STATUTORY AND NON-STATUTORY GUIDANCE

The teaching of reading is a statutory requirement in the UK. *Focus on Comprehension* has been developed against the backcloth of the statutory requirements of England and Wales, Scotland and Northern Ireland and the objectives of the National Literacy Project.

The National Curriculum for England and Wales

The National Curriculum expects that pupils' reading will be developed through the use of progressively more challenging and demanding tasks.

The General Requirements of the National Curriculum state that in order to develop as effective readers, pupils should be taught to:
- read accurately, fluently and with understanding;
- understand and respond to the texts they read;
- read, analyse and evaluate a wide range of texts, including literature from the English literary heritage and from other cultures and traditions.

At Key Stage 1, the Programmes of Study require that children should be taught to use phonic knowledge, graphic knowledge, word recognition, grammatical knowledge and contextual understanding along with opportunities to:
- talk about characters, events and language in books, beginning to use appropriate terminology;
- say what might happen next in a story;
- retell stories;
- explain the content of a passage;
- review their reading;
- read short texts including playscripts;
- hear stories and poems read aloud frequently and regularly;
- prepare, present and act out stories and poems they have read;
- consider the characteristics and features of different kinds of texts;
- use reference materials for different purposes, and should be taught about structural devices for organising information, such as contents, headings, captions.

Scottish 5-14 Guidelines

The Scottish 5-14 Guidelines include the following in their guidance to teachers:
- Learning to read accurately and with discrimination becomes increasingly important as pupils move through their education.
- The importance of meaning should be stressed at all stages.
- Reading should always have a purpose which is clear. Pupils must … learn to recognise the more common genres of fiction and non-fiction.
- The teacher needs to deploy a widening range of techniques such as sequencing, prediction, cloze procedure, evaluating the text, making deductions, comparing and contrasting different texts.
- Reading activities should demand that pupils show an overall grasp of a text, an understanding of specific details and how they contribute to the whole, make inferences, supply supporting evidence, and identify intended audience, purpose and features of style.
- Teaching strategies … will help them to make sense of aspects such as plot, characters and themes.
- The teacher can focus on texts:
  – by directing (pupils) into the task,
  – by providing questions which ask for literal, inferential and evaluative responses,
  – by asking them (pupils) to demonstrate understanding,
  – by asking readers to use the text as a model for their own writing.

Northern Ireland Curriculum

Focus on Comprehension follows the guidance to teachers addressed in The Northern Ireland Curriculum as shown below.

Pupils should have opportunities to:
- read … from an increasingly wide selection of books;
- discuss their comprehension and interpretation of the texts they have read, justifying their responses logically by inference, deduction and reference to evidence within the text;

Northern Ireland Curriculum continued

- learn that different reading purposes require different reading skills;
- acquire the use of skills necessary to locate information within texts;
- (use resources) making use of organisational devices to locate, select, evaluate and communicate information;
- discuss and consider aspects of stories, for example, characters, places, objects and events, paying attention to what is written and how it is expressed;
- discuss texts, exploring ways in which word meanings can be manipulated;
- reconsider their initial response to texts in the light of insight and information which subsequently emerge in their reading;
- encounter a wide variety of texts;
- respond with sensitivity to what they read, developing the ability to place themselves in someone else's position and extending their capacity for sympathy and empathy;
- speculate on situations read about, predict what may happen or consider what might have happened;
- discuss features of language.

The National Literacy Strategy

As well as taking into account the various UK statutory curriculum requirements, *Focus on Comprehension* has been designed to help schools meet the text level objectives of the National Literacy Strategy. *Focus on Comprehension* follows closely the range of texts and objectives for each year specified by the National Literacy Strategy.

The National Literacy Strategy characterises the literary primary-school pupil as one who is able to:

- read … with confidence, fluency and understanding;
- orchestrate a full range of reading cues … monitor their reading and correct their mistakes;
- have an interest in words and their meanings and a growing vocabulary;
- … understand and be familiar with some of the ways in which narratives are structured through basic literary ideas of setting, character and plot;
- understand and use … a wide range of non-fiction texts;
- have a suitable technical vocabulary through which to understand and discuss their reading;
- be interested in books, read with enjoyment and evaluate and justify their preferences;
- through reading … develop their powers of imagination, inventiveness and critical awareness.

COMPONENTS OF FOCUS ON COMPREHENSION

NLS Level	Course Book	Teacher's Book
1	Starter Book (24 pp)	Book 'A' (144 pp) for Starter and Introductory Books
2	Introductory Book (48 pp)	
3	Book 1 (48 pp)	Book 'B' (100 pp) for Books 1 and 2
4	Book 2 (48 pp)	
5	Book 3 (64 pp)	Book 'C' (100 pp) for Books 3 and 4
6	Book 4 (64 pp)	

STRUCTURE AND FEATURES

Pupils' Books
- Each book in the series is divided into 22 Teaching Units (single A4 pages of stimulus material in the Starter Book; double-pages in Introductory Book and Pupils' Books 1 and 2; two-, three- and four-page units in Pupils' Books 3 and 4).
- Each Teaching Unit is structured in the same way, in the Introductory Book through to Pupils' Book 4, in order to facilitate planning, provide differentiation, make pages easily accessible to pupils.
- Five sections appear in each unit, as follows:

  Think ahead
  - introduces the stimulus reading passage
  - poses open-ended questions for whole-class discussion
  - provides a clear purpose for reading the passage.

  The stimulus passage
  - provides the main text to work on
  - provides a wide range of fiction and non-fiction texts
  - provides progressively more challenging and demanding extracts
  - may be used for 'shared' or 'guided' reading.

  Thinking back
  - provides activities which encourage 'reading the lines', focusing mainly on literal comprehension
  - provides suitable activities for a whole class.

  Thinking about it
  - provides activities at an intermediate level
  - encourages 'reading between the lines', focusing mainly on reorganisation and inferential comprehension
  - provides activities appropriate for whole class, group or individual work.

  Thinking it through
  - provides activities at a third, and higher level of differentiation
  - encourages 'reading beyond the lines', focusing mainly on evaluative and appreciative comprehension
  - provides activities most appropriate for group and individual work.

The Starter Book
The Starter Book varies slightly in format from the other Pupils' Books.
- It is still structured into 22 Teaching Units, but each unit consists of just a 'Think ahead' section followed by a stimulus passage.
- The 'Thinking back', 'Thinking about it' and 'Thinking it through' activities are in the form of copymasters in the Teacher's Book.

Teacher's Book
The Teacher's Book:
- defines comprehension
- provides information on the aims, approach, and structure of the course
- sets *Focus on Comprehension* in the context of statutory curriculum guidance
- sets *Focus on Comprehension* in the context of the National Literacy Strategy
- provides practical advice on organising and using *Focus on Comprehension* with special reference to the Literacy Hour
- provides detailed answers to each unit
- provides a comprehensive range of further teaching ideas on how to use each unit for further text level activities (in comprehension and writing composition), sentence level and word level work.
- includes accompanying photocopiable activities for each unit
- provides class and individual record sheets and practical assessment suggestions.

Copymasters in Teacher's Books
- Each unit in the Starter Book has three accompanying copymasters (in this Teacher's Book 'A') in the form of 'Thinking back', 'Thinking about it' and 'Thinking it through' activities which provide for different levels of comprehension related to each stimulus passage.
- However, each unit in the Introductory Book and Pupils' Books 1–4 has one accompanying copymaster which:
  - develops or extends the theme or type of activity in the main unit
  - provides a range of activities which may not be appropriate in a textbook format
  - provides extracts for comparison or poems/passages by the same poet/author
  - provides playlets or poems for performance.
- The copymasters may be used alongside the main unit or independently.
- They may be used for whole class, group or individual work.
- They may be used for homework assignments.

OVERVIEW OF RANGE OF TEXTS

Starter Book

Fiction and poetry
Stories with familiar settings; stories, rhymes and poems with familiar, predictable and repetitive patterns, and structures for our culture and other cultures; traditional stories and rhymes; fairy stories; stories based on fantasy worlds; poems with similar themes; plays.

Non-fiction
Signs; labels; captions; lists; instructions; information books and texts; simple dictionaries.

Introductory Book

Fiction and poetry
Stories and poems with familiar settings; traditional stories; stories and poems from other cultures; stories and poems with predictable and patterned language; poems and stories by significant children's poets and authors; texts with language play.

Non-fiction
Instructions; alphabetically ordered texts; explanations; information books including non-chronological reports.

Book 1

Fiction and poetry
Stories with familiar settings; plays; myths, legends, fables; traditional stories; adventure and mystery stories; poems based on observation and the senses; shape poems; oral and performance poetry; humorous poems; poetry with language play.

Non-fiction
Information books; non-chronological reports; thesaurus/dictionary; instructions; letters.

Book 2

Fiction and poetry
Historical texts and poems; plays; imagined works; sci-fi/fantasy; dilemmas and issues; stories and poems from other cultures; classic poetry; modern poetry; range of poetic forms.

Non-fiction
Newspaper/magazine reports; instructions; information texts; explanations; persuasive writing; discussion texts.

Book 3

Fiction and poetry
Stories by significant children's authors; traditional stories and poems from other cultures; plays; concrete poetry; classic poetry; narrative poetry; choral and performance poetry.

Non-fiction
Recounts; observational records and reports; instructional texts; explanations; persuasive writing.

Book 4

Fiction and poetry
Classic fiction, poetry and drama; TV/film adaptations; range of genres; range of poetry.

Non-fiction
Autobiography/biography; journalistic writing; reports; discussion texts; formal writing; explanations; reference texts.

Scope and range of individual books

The range of texts is summarised at the front of each of the pupils' books in the form of a scope and sequence chart. This shows the range of texts covered within the fiction and non-fiction categories.

USING *FOCUS ON COMPREHENSION* IN THE CLASSROOM

Focus on Comprehension and the Literacy Hour

Focus on Comprehension has been designed with the National Literacy Project very much in mind. Because it follows closely the range of texts and objectives for each year specified in the framework document, it has great potential for supporting schools teaching the daily Literacy Hour.

Class work

The National Literacy Strategy defines 'shared' reading as a class activity using a common text, such as a text extract in which the teacher reads to and with the class, modelling and discussing texts. *Focus on Comprehension* provides a range of progressively more challenging and demanding extracts and differentiated comprehension questions.

The extract could be shared with the class and discussed, using some of the activities in the Pupils' Books for discussion or written comprehension responses. (The 'Further Teaching Opportunities' section in the Teacher's Book provides additional suggestions for comprehension work.)

The use of the passage may be extended further to provide related writing composition activities, and classwork arising from the texts at sentence and word level. The 'Further Teaching Opportunities' section of each unit's lesson notes provides for this.

Group work

'Guided' reading is when the teacher focuses on independent reading. The framework document suggests that it should be 'a carefully structured group activity, involving time for sustained reading. Pupils should have individual copies of the same text. The texts need to be carefully selected to match the reading levels of the group.' The structure of the *Focus on Comprehension* books makes them ideal for this purpose. The differentiated comprehension activities provide 'questions to direct or check up on the reading, points to note, problems to solve', and so on, which meet the text level objectives in the framework. The teacher could introduce the text to the group (to familiarise them with overall context, and to point out key words) as appropriate, use the differentiated activities to assess the development of comprehension and offer support to each pupil as required. The copymasters for each unit provide further opportunities for this too.

Independent work

Irrespective of whether *Focus on Comprehension* is used for shared and/or guided reading, it also offers enormous potential for additional independent work. The framework document suggests that 'independent tasks could cover a wide range of objectives including comprehension work, independent writing, vocabulary extension and dictionary work, practice and investigations in grammar, punctuation and sentence construction, phonic and spelling investigations and practice'. Children may be asked to complete some of the activity sections following each unit or the related copymasters at this time for additional comprehension work. The 'Further Teaching Opportunities' section of each unit's lesson notes provides numerous ideas for capitalising on the extract in each unit at text, sentence and word level for independent work.

Assessment and record-keeping

A systematic use of the *Focus on Comprehension* course will help children prepare for the statutory and non-statutory assessment requirements.

The tightly-structured nature of the reading material and the differentiated range of comprehension activities help make the ongoing assessment of the children's reading and comprehension skills easy to monitor. It may be considered desirable to ask children to complete one of the units each term (and/or one of the accompanying copymasters) on separate sheets of paper, to keep in their individual portfolios as markers and records of progress and achievement.

Recording pupils' progress is an important aspect of classroom management and good educational practice. Two record sheets are provided. The Class Record Sheet (see page 10) enables you to maintain an overview on class progress as a whole, whereas the Individual Record Sheet (on page 11) enables you to monitor individual progress and achievement.

CLASS RECORD SHEET

Book _____   **Class** _____

Name	\multicolumn{22}{c}{Units}

Name	1	2	3	4	5	6	7	8	9	10	11	12	13	14	15	16	17	18	19	20	21	22

Note: It is suggested that a pupil's progress for each unit is indicated as follows:
/ = attempted;   × = completed satisfactorily

INDIVIDUAL RECORD SHEET

Name _____ **Book** _____ **Class** _____

Unit	Comment	Date
1		
2		
3		
4		
5		
6		
7		
8		
9		
10		
11		
12		
13		
14		
15		
16		
17		
18		
19		
20		
21		
22		

Focus on Comprehension Teacher's Book 'A'. Text © Louis Fidge 1999
Published by Thomas Nelson and Sons Ltd 1999

UNIT 1 Get Me Out!

Starter Book

FURTHER TEACHING OPPORTUNITIES

Text level

Reading comprehension
- When reading the unit, discuss each picture and text, one at a time. Encourage children to notice the repetitive patterning of the language and to join in where they are able.
- Use the picture cues to help support the reading of the text. Guess each time whether there are sufficient animals to pull Elephant out.
- Draw attention to the sound Elephant makes, coming out of the water. What sound would he have made falling in?
- Discuss how Elephant would have felt at the end of the story.
- Re-enact the story. This could lead to a further discussion on the size and relative strength of each individual character.

Writing composition
- Encourage children to write about an experience they have had in water.
- Children could use the story as a model for writing something similar about other animals, such as 'The day Henry the Hippo got stuck in the mud'.

Sentence level

Grammatical awareness
- Use the predictability and patterning of the language to encourage children to read the text independently, with appropriate expression and intonation.
- Point out the use of the prepositions 'in' and 'out'. Use other positional words in a practical way, relating them to things in the classroom.
- Ask children to suggest things that go 'up' (and things that come down!).

Sentence construction and punctuation
- Whilst reading, encourage children to take note of full stops at the ends of sentences. Note too, how the name of each character begins with a capital letter. Relate this to children's own names.
- Draw attention to the use of speech marks to show when the characters speak.

Word level

Phonics, word recognition and spelling
- Use the word 'in' in the text for word-building practice. Ask children to use analogy to build other 'in' words. What different onsets may be used in front of it for making other words?
- Have a 'high frequency word' hunt. Give children a couple of high frequency words and see how many they can find in the text, such as 'said, the'.

Vocabulary extension
- Brainstorm, and list, the names of other wild animals that could have been in the story.
- Talk about other games or activities that require more than one person to play or do.

ANSWERS

Thinking back
1 Elephant 2 Tiger 3 Crocodile
4 Monkey 5 Snake

Thinking about it
The six pictures should be sequenced to tell the story.

Thinking it through
Elephant fell in the river.
First, Tiger tried to pull Elephant out.
Next, Crocodile pulled Tiger.
Then Monkey pulled Crocodile.
Last of all, Snake pulled Monkey.
They all pulled Elephant out of the river.

UNIT 1 Get Me Out!

Thinking back

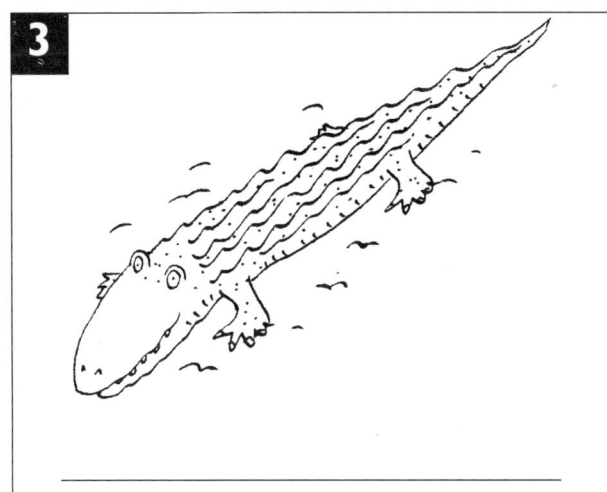

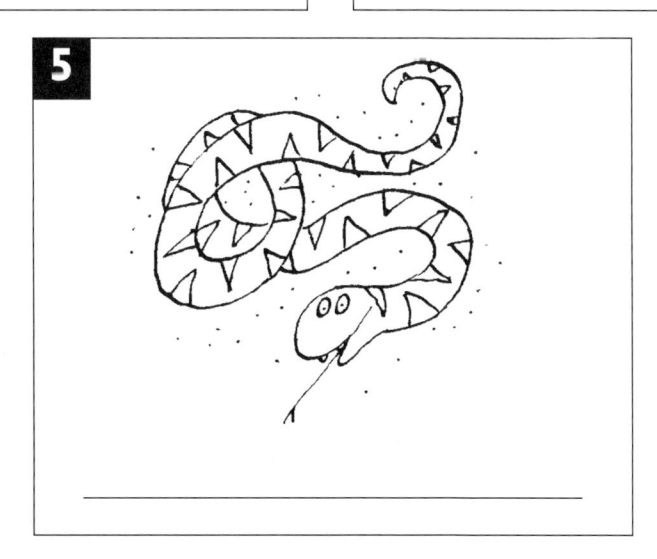

Name _____ Date _____

Label each picture correctly.

| Monkey | Elephant | Snake | Tiger | Crocodile |

1.
2.
3.
4.
5.

Focus on Comprehension Teacher's Book 'A'. Text © Louis Fidge 1999
Illustrations © Nelson 1999. Published by Thomas Nelson and Sons Ltd 1999

Starter book / Copymaster / Unit 1

UNIT 1 Get Me Out!

Thinking about it

Name _____   Date _____

Cut out the pictures.
Put them in the correct order to tell the story.

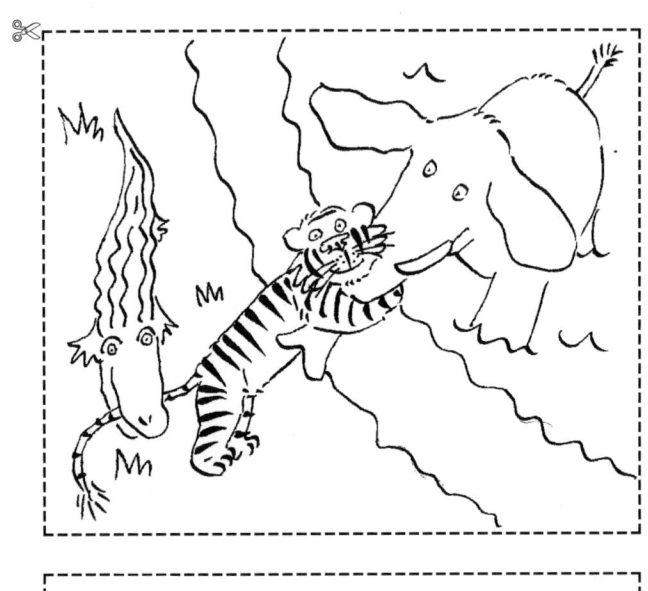

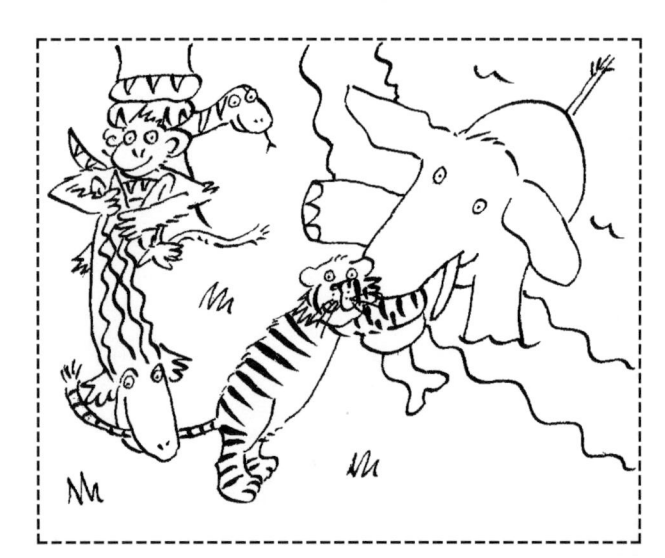

Starter Book / Copymaster / Unit 1
14

Focus on Comprehension Teacher's Book 'A'. Text © Louis Fidge 1999
Illustrations © Nelson 1999. Published by Thomas Nelson and Sons Ltd 1999

UNIT 1 Get Me Out!

Thinking it through

Name _____ Date _____

**Cut out the sentences.
Put them in order to tell the story.**

They all pulled Elephant out of the river.

Next, Crocodile pulled Tiger.

Elephant fell in the river.

Last of all, Snake pulled Monkey.

Then Monkey pulled Crocodile.

First, Tiger tried to pull Elephant out.

UNIT 2 Sam's Busy Week
Starter Book

FURTHER TEACHING OPPORTUNITIES

Text level

Reading comprehension
- Before reading the story encourage children to talk about the things they do regularly each week.
- Read the caption under the first picture. If possible have the rest of the page covered up. Discuss the purpose of a library and children's experiences of using one.
- Read the rest of the unit, discussing each picture and text, one at a time. Discuss what Sam did each day. Notice how Sam is getting tireder as the week goes on. Discuss the reasons for this.
- Encourage children to notice the repetitive patterning of the language and to join in where they are able. Use the picture cues to help support the reading of the text.

Writing composition
- Encourage the children to discuss and write about an eventful week they have had. What happened?
- Use the format of the story as a model for writing their own story along the same lines, changing the places visited each day.
- Alternatively the theme could be adapted and changed. It could lend itself to a simple diary 'story'. Each picture and caption could be written on a separate sheet of paper and stapled together to make a storybook. Children could add details such as covers, a title, author's name, as a way into discussing book conventions.

Sentence level

Grammatical awareness
- Encourage children to use as many cues as possible when reading the text to help unlock the meaning of unknown words.
- Present children with some of the words in the sentences in the wrong order and ask them to resequence them correctly.

Sentence construction and punctuation
- Use the word 'sentence' in discussions. Notice that they always begin with a capital letter. Have a full stop hunt. Where do full stops come?

Word level

Phonics, word recognition and spelling
- Use the story as a way of focusing on the spelling and sequencing of the days of the week. Why are the days all written with capital letters?
- Use some of the words in the text as a starting point for experimenting with rhyming such as 'Sam', 'ham', 'jam', 'ram'.
- Experiment with changing the onsets of words such as change the 'p' of 'park' to a 'b', 'd', 'h', 'l', 'm', 'sh'.
- Look for high frequency words in the text such as 'went, to, the'. Use them in different contexts in other made-up sentences.

Vocabulary extension
- Introduce the names and spellings of the months of the year and sequence them correctly.

ANSWERS

Thinking back
Children have to draw pictures showing what Sam did each day:
On Monday Sam went to the library.
On Tuesday Sam went to the park.
On Wednesday Sam went to the zoo.
On Thursday Sam went to the swimming pool.
On Friday Sam went to the cinema.
On Saturday Sam went to the shops.
On Sunday Sam had a rest.

Thinking about it
Children have to fill in the correct day in each sentence.
On Wednesday Sam went to the zoo.
On Saturday Sam went to the shops.
On Monday Sam went to the library.
On Friday Sam went to the cinema.
On Tuesday Sam went to the park.
On Thursday she went to the swimming pool.
Lastly children have to sequence pictures in correct order (see Thinking Back).

Thinking it through
Children have to sequence the sentence in correct order. Sam went to the park.
Children then draw or write what they think happened at the park. (open answers)

UNIT 2 Sam's Busy Week

Thinking back

Name _____ Date _____

Draw a picture of what Sam did each day.

On Monday

On Tuesday

On Wednesday

On Thursday

On Friday

On Saturday

On Sunday

Focus on Comprehension Teacher's Book 'A'. Text © Louis Fidge 1999
Published by Thomas Nelson and Sons Ltd 1999

Starter Book / Copymaster / Unit 2

UNIT 2 Sam's Busy Week

Thinking about it

Name _____ Date _____

Fill in the correct day in each gap.

| Monday | Tuesday | Wednesday |
| Thursday | Friday | Saturday |

On _____
Sam went to the zoo.

On _____
Sam went to the shops.

On _____
Sam went to the library.

On _____
Sam went to the cinema.

On _____
Sam went to the park.

On _____ Sam went to the swimming pool.

Now cut out the pictures and sentences.
Put them in the correct order.

Starter Book / Copymaster / Unit 2

Focus on Comprehension Teacher's Book 'A'. Text © Louis Fidge 1999
Illustrations © Nelson 1999. Published by Thomas Nelson and Sons Ltd 1999

UNIT 2 Sam's Busy Week

Thinking it through

Name _____ Date _____

Write the words in the correct order.

went   Sam   to   park.   the

Sam _____ .

Draw or write what you think happened at the park.

UNIT 3 A Number Rhyme

Starter Book

FURTHER TEACHING OPPORTUNITIES

Text level

Reading comprehension
- Before reading the rhyme, ask children if they know any number rhymes: for example, One, two, buckle my shoe.
- This rhyme is also an action rhyme. Encourage the children to follow the instructions to reinforce the meaning of the words.
- Extemporise on the pattern of the rhyme by asking children to substitute other words for the rhyming words: for example, Number one, lie in the sun, eat a bun, go for a run, have some fun.

Writing composition
- Turn the last idea into a class rhyme, by writing suggestions on the board. Use it as an opportunity for drawing attention to rhyme and spelling patterns. Children could also use it for handwriting practice too. The rhyme could be made into a concertina book or long frieze for display purposes.

Sentence level

Grammatical awareness
- Children must learn to expect texts to make sense. Re-read the rhyme again, but make some deliberate mistakes. For example, insert the wrong number word, or insert a word that doesn't rhyme. Ask children to articulate what is wrong and explain why.
- When the rhyme is familiar to children, ask them to read it aloud with appropriate expression and intonation (especially the last line!).

Sentence construction and punctuation
- This rhyme is written as ten separate sentences. Notice how each sentence begins with the same word and discuss why it always has a capital letter. Notice that nine of the sentences end with full stops. Explain their purpose. If appropriate, name the exclamation mark and demonstrate what signal this gives to the reader in how to say the sentence.

Word level

Phonics, word recognition and spelling
- Have some fun using the words for experimenting with rhyme. Brainstorm and list words that rhyme, identifying and sorting those words which sound and are written the same, such as three, tree, see, bee and those words which sound the same but have a different letter pattern, such as tea, sea, me, we, the, pea.

Vocabulary extension
- Extend the work on number words to include higher numbers (for instance, numbers to twenty, other big numbers they know).

ANSWERS

Thinking back
Children write the correct number under each picture.

Thinking about it
Children have to put pictures and sentences in the correct order.
Number one, touch your tongue.
Number two, touch your shoe.
Number three, touch your knee.
Number four, touch the floor.
Number five, learn to jive.
Number six, pick up sticks.
Number seven, point to heaven.
Number eight, shut the gate.
Number nine, touch your spine.
Number ten, do it again!

Thinking it through
One little monkey climbing a tree.
Two little monkeys splashing in the sea.
Three little monkeys playing on a swing.
Four little monkeys dancing in a ring.
Five little monkeys drinking lemonade.
Six little monkeys digging with a spade.
Seven little monkeys chasing pussy cats.
Eight little monkeys wearing funny hats.
Nine little monkeys nodding little heads.
Ten little monkeys sleeping in their beds.

UNIT 3 A Number Rhyme

Thinking back

Name _____   Date _____

Write the correct number under each picture.

| one   two   three   four   five   six   seven   eight   nine   ten |

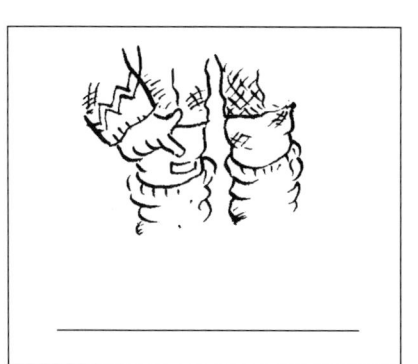

Now practise the rhyme and say it to a friend.

UNIT 3 A Number Rhyme

Thinking about it

Name _____ Date _____

**Cut out the pictures and sentences.
Put them in the correct order.**

Number three, touch your knee.	Number one, touch your tongue.
Number nine, touch your spine.	Number four, touch the floor.
Number seven, point to heaven.	Number six, pick up sticks.
Number two, touch your shoe.	Number eight, shut the gate.
Number ten, do it again!	Number five, learn to jive.

Starter Book / Copymaster / Unit 3
22

Focus on Comprehension Teacher's Book 'A'. Text © Louis Fidge 1999
Illustrations © Nelson 1999. Published by Thomas Nelson and Sons Ltd 1999

UNIT 3 A Number Rhyme

Thinking it through

Name _____ Date _____

Choose the correct word to finish each sentence.

(sea, tree)
One little monkey climbing a __tree__ .

(sea, tree)
Two little monkeys splashing in the _____ .

(swing, ring)
Three little monkeys playing on a _____ .

(swing, ring)
Four little monkeys dancing in a _____ .

(lemonade, spade)
Five little monkeys drinking _____ .

(lemonade, spade)
Six little monkeys digging with a _____ .

(hats, cats)
Seven little monkeys chasing pussy _____ .

(hats, cats)
Eight little monkeys wearing funny _____ .

UNIT 4 The Puddle in the Park

Starter Book

FURTHER TEACHING OPPORTUNITIES

Text level

Reading comprehension
- Ask children to talk about visits they have made to the park. What is there to do in your local park? Have the children had any similar accidents to the child in the story?
- Look at the title of the unit. Notice the alliterative element.
- Look at and discuss each picture one at a time, masking the text. What can be learnt or inferred from just the pictures? (Make the point that usually pictures and text go together to provide meaning.)
- Read the story to and with the children, encouraging the children to discuss what they notice, such as the fact that basically each caption is the same, with the exception of a word or two.
- Where does the story take place? How does the child feel in each picture? Ask the children to suggest why the child doesn't notice the puddle at the bottom of the slide.
- What do the children think the child does next?

Writing composition
- Use the unit as a model for further park-based stories such as hiring a boat on the lake, sailing a model boat, feeding the ducks.
- Children could be encouraged to write simple sentences about accidents they have had and a class Accident Book could be compiled.

Sentence level

Grammatical awareness
- Read the story again but substitute words so the captions do not make sense such as substitute 'swing' for 'slide', or play about with the order of the words and ask children to explain what is wrong.
- Provide children with the words for the first sentence in the wrong order and ask them to sequence the words correctly so they make sense.

Sentence construction and punctuation
- Use the sentence 'I went on the swing' to introduce position words. Provide children with other position words such as 'under', 'above', 'up', 'through', 'behind' and ask children to suggest sentences containing each. Use this to reinforce the conventions of sentence structure such as having capital letters to begin and full stops to end each sentence.

Word level

Phonics, word recognition and spelling
- Use the words 'swing', 'slide', 'seesaw' from the text to focus on initial letter sounds. Think of other words beginning with the 's' sound. Compare the difference between 'on' and 'in'.
- Make some words using 'in' as a rime, by adding different onsets such as 'bin', 'din', 'fin', 'pin', 'tin', 'win', 'chin', 'shin'. Allow this to extend to work on other rimes as appropriate. Do some work on final letter sounds. Compare the final letter sounds of 'bin' and 'bit'.
- The unit contains several high frequency words like 'I', 'went', 'on', 'the'. Identify and find all the examples of these in the text, and in other texts.

Vocabulary extension
- Use the story to introduce other words related to the park such as 'grass, ducks, lake, gate'.

ANSWERS

Thinking back
1 This is the seesaw.
2 This is the climbing frame.
3 This is the slide.
4 This is the swing.
5 This is the puddle.
6 This is the roundabout.

Thinking about it
1 I went on the swing.
2 I went on the seesaw.
3 I went on the roundabout.
4 I went on the climbing frame.
5 I went on the slide.
6 I went in the puddle!

Thinking it through
(open answers)

UNIT 4 The Puddle in the Park — Thinking back

Name _____   Date _____

Finish the sentences.

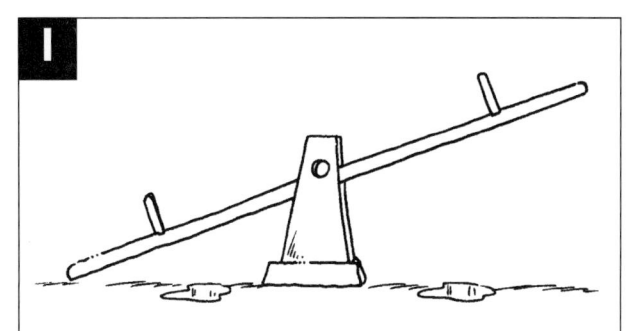

1

Is this the swing or the seesaw?

This is _____ .

2

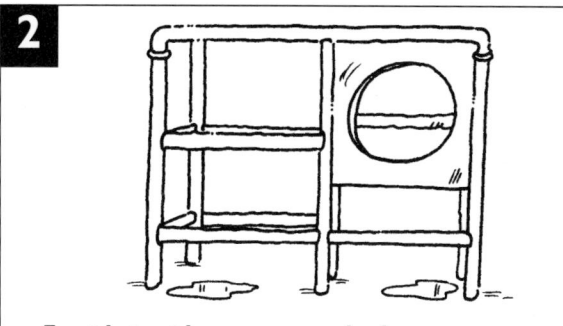

Is this the roundabout or the climbing frame?

This is _____ .

3

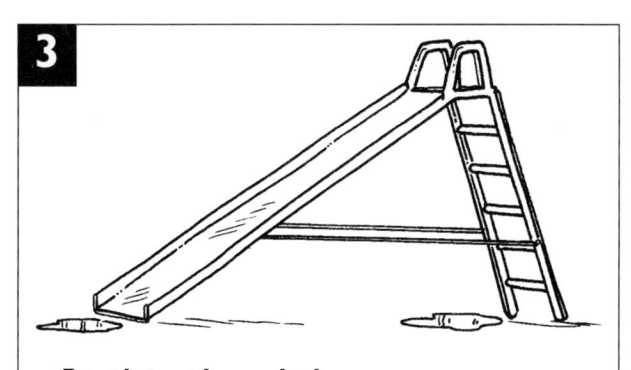

Is this the slide or the roundabout?

This is _____ .

4

Is this the swing or the slide?

This is _____ .

5

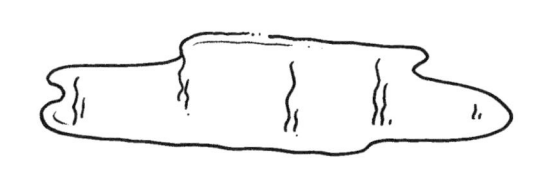

Is this the roundabout or the puddle?

This is _____ .

6

Is this the puddle or the roundabout?

This is _____ .

UNIT 4 The Puddle in the Park
Thinking about it

Name _____ Date _____

> Cut out the pictures and sentences.
> Put them in the correct order.
> Find the answers on page 6 of your book.

I went on the roundabout.

I went on the slide.

I went on the swing.

I went in the puddle!

I went on the seesaw.

I went on the climbing frame.

Starter Book / Copymaster / Unit 4

Focus on Comprehension Teacher's Book 'A'. Text © Louis Fidge 1999
Illustrations © Nelson 1999. Published by Thomas Nelson and Sons Ltd 1999

UNIT 4 The Puddle in the Park *Thinking it through*

Name _____   Date _____

What will my Mum say when I get home?

What will happen to me? Draw a picture or write a sentence.

UNIT 5 Let's Make a Shaker

Starter Book

FURTHER TEACHING OPPORTUNITIES

Text level

Reading comprehension
- Read the title of the unit. Ask children what they think the unit is going to be about. Is it going to be a story? a rhyme? some instructions?
- Look at each section one at a time. Firstly read the sub-heading and then look at and discuss each picture. Read the caption for each picture, drawing attention to the way the picture and text interact in providing context and meaning, and help especially with unlocking the meaning of harder words (such as replace), or unknown words.
- When the text has been read and discussed, look back at the way the unit is structured into three sections. How does this help? For example, why does the 'what you need' section come first?

Writing composition
- If possible, allow each child to follow the instructions and make his/her own shaker. This reinforces the functional value of the text.
- Extend this to looking at other instructional texts (such as simple recipes).
- Read and use and draw attention to captions, lists and signs in the classroom and around the school at every opportunity.

Sentence level

Grammatical awareness
- Provide children with a range of pictures, such as a house or car and ask them to think of simple captions for each.
- Encourage them to bring in photos and to write a sentence under each: such as 'This is me when I was a baby'. Encourage children to use capitals at the beginning of their sentences (and when using the pronoun 'I', and full stops at the end).
- Provide children with a simple story told in three pictures and to ask them match an appropriate sentence with each picture.

Sentence construction and punctuation
- Look back at the captions under the pictures in the unit. Which are sentences and which are not? Draw attention to the fact that a sentence begins with a capital letter and usually ends with a full stop.

Word level

Phonics, word recognition and spelling
- Use the words 'can' and 'lid' from the text as a starting point for focusing on segmenting and blending CVC words, thinking of others with the same patterns and doing some work on rhyming.
- This could be extended to brainstorming other words from the same family; for example, as shake (make, bake), rice (nice, mice), dry (sky, why), play (may, bay), name (same, game).
- There are many opportunities to study interesting features of different words.

Vocabulary extension
- How many musical instruments can the children name? How are they played? Are they blown, struck, shaken, plucked? What sound do they make? What are they made of?

ANSWERS

Thinking back
In order to make a shaker you need:
some dry rice, a plastic bottle with a lid, a funnel

Thinking about it
Take the lid off the bottle.
Pour the rice into the bottle.
Put the lid back on the bottle.
Shake the bottle.

Thinking it through
What you need: some water, a stick, four glass bottles
What you do: Fill each bottle to a different level.
How you play it: Tap the bottles with the stick.

UNIT 5 Let's Make a Shaker

Thinking back

Name _____ Date _____

Find the answers on pupils' book page 7.

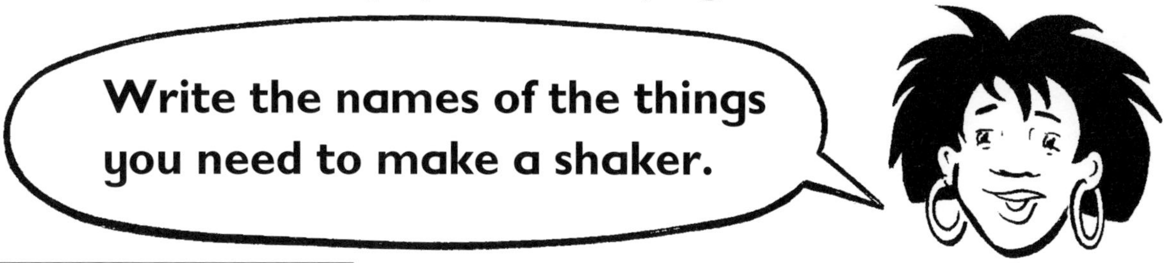

Write the names of the things you need to make a shaker.

1 _____

2 _____

3 _____

UNIT 5 Let's Make a Shaker

Thinking about it

Name _____   Date _____

Write the correct sentence by each picture.

| Shake the bottle. | Put the lid back on the bottle. |
| Pour the rice into the bottle. | Take the lid off the bottle. |

1 _____

2 _____

3 _____

4 _____

Starter Book / Copymaster / Unit 5

UNIT 5 Let's Make a Shaker

Thinking it through

Name _____ Date _____

Here are the instructions for making a glass xylophone, but they are all muddled up.

What you need:
Write the correct labels under each picture.

| four glass bottles | some water | a stick |

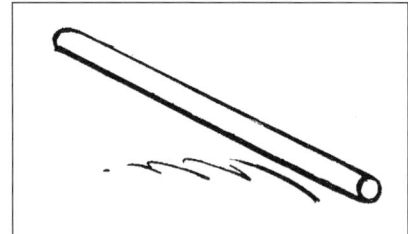

What you do:
Write the words in the correct order.

each bottle Fill to a level. different

How you play it:
Write the words in the correct order.

bottles Tap the stick. with the

UNIT 6 Miss Polly had a Dolly

Starter Book

FURTHER TEACHING OPPORTUNITIES

Text level

Reading comprehension
- Introduce the unit by asking children for their anecdotal experiences of being ill; for example, calling the doctor, being confined to bed, taking medicine, feeling unwell, names of illnesses, having visitors, being fussed over.
- Read the rhyme through, several times, pointing out the relationship with the pictures and emphasising the rhyming elements.
- After reading ask some who, what, where, when-type questions to check literal understanding of the rhyme and to establish details about the setting, characters and events, such as Who had a dolly? What was the matter with it?
- Children will enjoy acting out the rhyme as it is said. Try some choral speaking and get different groups to be responsible for saying different verses.

Writing composition
- Reproduce the rhyme with key rhyming words missing. Encourage children to apply grammatical, phonic and sight vocabulary skills to supply and spell the missing words correctly.
- Have fun changing the words slightly, such as Miss Pat had a cat, She called for the vet, and so on.

Sentence level

Grammatical awareness
- During the reading of the rhyme, encourage the children to begin contributing words by pausing at key places and allowing children to supply the missing word/s (this works especially well with missing rhyming words).
- When reading the rhyme, help children pay attention to the meaning and punctuation by using appropriate expression and intonation.

Sentence construction and punctuation
- Write out the rhyme as sentences, making appropriate changes, such as Miss Polly had a dolly who was sick. She called for the doctor. Cut these up and ask children to sequence them correctly. Discuss the features of sentences; for example, they begin with capital letters and usually end with full stops.

Word level

Phonics, word recognition and spelling
- Use the rhyming words as starting points. Brainstorm and list other words that rhyme with these. Sort the words according to whether they look and sound the same or whether they have different letter patterns such as bed, red, fed, wed – and dead, said.
- Use some of the words to stress initial and final letter sounds, such as the difference between red and bed, and bed and bet.
- Select a number of high frequency words and ask children to find them in the rhyme.

Vocabulary extension
- Think of words with similar meanings linked to words from the text, such as sick – ill, unwell, hurt; bag – basket, box, holdall, purse; knock – tap, hit, bash.
- List words associated with doctors, illnesses, hospitals.

ANSWERS

Thinking back
Children have to match the correct picture to each verse of the rhyme.

Thinking about it
Children have to fill in the missing rhyming words from the poem.
Words rhyming with sick: tick, lick, pick, quick
Words rhyming with hat: cat, mat, bat, fat
Words rhyming with head: bed, red, fed
Words rhyming with pill: bill, fill, hill

Thinking it through
Children have to complete the missing lines from Incy Wincy Spider:
Incy Wincy Spider climbed the water spout.
Down came the rain and washed poor Incy out.
Out came the sun, and dried up all the rain.
Incy Wincy Spider climbed up the spout again.

UNIT 6 Miss Polly had a Dolly

Thinking back

Name _____ Date _____

**Cut out the pictures at the bottom of the page.
Match each picture to the correct verse of the rhyme.**

Miss Polly had a dolly
Who was sick, sick, sick.
So she called for the doctor
To be quick, quick, quick.

The doctor came
With his bag and his hat,
And he knocked on the door
With a rat tat tat.

He looked at the dolly
And he shook his head.
Then he said, "Miss Polly,
Put her to bed, bed, bed."

Out of his bag
He took a pill, pill, pill,
And said, "I'll be back in the morning
With my bill, bill, bill."

UNIT 6 Miss Polly had a Dolly

Thinking about it

Name _____   Date _____

Fill in the missing rhyming words.

Miss Polly had a dolly
Who was sick, sick, sick.
So she called for the doctor
To be _____ , _____ , _____ .

The doctor came
With his bag and his hat,
And he knocked on the door
With a _____ , _____ , _____ .

He looked at the dolly
And he shook his head.
Then he said, "Miss Polly,
Put her to _____ , _____ , _____ ."

Out of his bag
He took a pill, pill, pill,
And said, "I'll be back in the morning
With my _____ , _____ , _____ ."

Colour red the words that rhyme with **sick**.

Colour blue the words that rhyme with **hat**.

tick	bed	cat
bill	mat	red	lick
fed	bat	fill
pick	hill	quick	fat

Colour yellow the words that rhyme with **head**.

Colour green the words that rhyme with **pill**.

Starter Book / Copymaster / Unit 6

UNIT 6 Miss Polly had a Dolly   *Thinking it through*

Name _____   Date _____

Put each line in the correct place to finish the rhyme.

| Climbed up the spout again. | And washed poor Incy out. |
| And dried up all the rain. | Climbed the water spout. |

Incy Wincy Spider
_____

Down came the rain
_____

Out came the sun,
_____

Incy Wincy Spider
_____

UNIT 7 The Gingerbread Man

Starter Book

FURTHER TEACHING OPPORTUNITIES

Text level

Reading comprehension
- Before looking at the unit ask children if they know the story of the Gingerbread Man. Encourage them to retell it in their own words.
- Look at the way the unit is presented (it is set out as a play). Explain this convention to children and show how different parts of the story are read by the different characters in it.
- After reading ask some who, what, where, when-type questions to check literal understanding of the story and to establish details about the setting, characters and events.
- Do the children know of any other stories with foxes in? Are foxes always depicted in a particular way?
- When they are familiar with the text, encourage different children to read and act out the different parts of the play.

Writing composition
- As a class, retell and write a simple version of the whole story, as a concertina book or frieze for the wall. Encourage the use of stock phrases such as 'once upon a time'.
- Ask children what they thought of the gingerbread man and the fox. What were they like? How did they behave? How would they describe each? Draw a picture of each and record characteristics and appearance, using single words, phrases or sentences.

Sentence level

Grammatical awareness
- Encourage children to offer alternative words to some of the words in the text that will still make sense, such as 'I will take (carry, help) you across the river.'

Sentence construction and punctuation
- When reading, ask children to point out full stops and capital letters and to use the term 'sentence' correctly. Draw attention to the fact that the personal pronoun 'I' is always written with a capital letter.

Word level

Phonics, word recognition and spelling
- Use the following words from the text to stimulate work on word endings, by suggesting and writing others with similar endings: cro*ss*, wi*ll*, ba*ck*, goi*ng*.
- There are several words in the text that introduce, and could lead into further work on, initial consonant blends, for example *st*ory, *sl*y, *sw*im, *cl*imbed, *br*ead. Brainstorm and write other words beginning with these clusters. Extend this to other consonant clusters at the beginnings of words.
- Select a number of high frequency words and ask children to find them in the text. Look at each word one at a time, and discuss any special features, such as 'too' has a double 'oo'; 'me', 'he' and 'the' all have a similar pattern; there is a 'hen' in 'then'. Use the 'Look, Say, Cover, Write, Check' method for learning each word.

Vocabulary extension
- Children could draw and use captions to label the parts of a fox's or the gingerbread man's body.
- How many synonyms for 'eat' can the children suggest (such as gobble, gulp, chew)?

ANSWERS

Thinking back

the fox	the gingerbread man
the gingerbread man	the fox
the gingerbread man	the fox

Thinking about it

1. the little old man; the little old lady; the hen; the cow; the horse
2. Because they wanted to eat him.
3. a river
4. a fox
5. He ate him up.
6. He was sly.

Thinking it through

(open answer)
The children have to think of a different ending for the story.

UNIT 7 The Gingerbread Man

Thinking back

Name _____ Date _____

Write down who said each thing.

the fox

the gingerbread man

1. I will take you across the river.

2. I'm on your tail.

3. Swim across the river, now.

4. Sit on my nose.

5. Now I can see where we are going.

6. Gobble! Gobble! Gulp!

UNIT 7 The Gingerbread Man
Thinking about it

Name _____   Date _____

Tick ✓ the best answers.

1 Who was the gingerbread man running away from?

the little old man ✓   the little old lady ☐   the hen ☐

the cow ☐   the horse ☐   the fox ☐

2 Why was the gingerbread man running away from everyone?

Because they wanted to eat him. ☐

Because they wanted to cook him. ☐

3 What was in his way?

a river ☐   a house ☐   a fox ☐

4 Who said he would help the gingerbread man?

a cow ☐   a fox ☐   a man ☐

5 What did the fox do to the gingerbread man?

He hugged him. ☐   He sang to him. ☐

He ate him up. ☐

6 What was the fox like?

He was sly. ☐   He was old. ☐   He was kind. ☐

UNIT 7 The Gingerbread Man — *Thinking it through*

Name _____ Date _____

Think of a good ending for this sentence.

The sly old fox tossed the gingerbread man up in the air and

_____

Make up a different ending for the story, so I don't get eaten! Draw a picture.

UNIT 8 The Princess and the Pea

Starter Book

FURTHER TEACHING OPPORTUNITIES

Text level

Reading comprehension

- Explain that this story is a fairy tale. Ask children to name any other fairy stories they know.
- If possible, mask the text of the story. Look at and discuss each picture one at a time. What can be learnt from just the pictures? (These will give some idea of the context of the story, the characters and events in it.)
- Read the text to and with the children. Point out how helpful the pictures can be.
- Ask children to retell the story, noticing the differences between the oral version and the written text.
- Discuss reasons for particular incidents in the story, such as Why did the prince put a pea under the mattresses?
- Discuss the way the story opens and ends – 'once upon a time' and 'they lived happily ever after'. Do the children know any other stories which begin and end like this?

Writing composition

- Ask the children to draw a picture of either the prince or the princess. Ask them to write some words, phrases or sentences under their picture about the character they have drawn.

Sentence level

Grammatical awareness

- Mask a few words in the text and ask children to read the text and guess what the missing words might be: for example, Once upon a _____ there lived a _____ who wanted to marry a princess.

Sentence construction and punctuation

- Draw children's attention to the fact that a line of print does not always equal a sentence (by reference to the captions under the pictures).
- Notice what the characters say is sometimes represented in speech bubbles.

Word level

Phonics, word recognition and spelling

- Use the word 'small' from the text. Ask children to suggest other words ending in 'll'. For instance, how many 'all', 'ill', 'ell', 'oll' and 'ull' words can be made? Do the same for 'ss' as in 'princess'.
- The word 'prince' may be used to stimulate work on initial consonant blends. How many 'pr' words can be thought of? Extend this to work on 'br', 'cr', 'dr', 'fr', 'gr', 'tr'. Make up silly sentences containing the words; for example, The proud prince picked the prize primroses.
- Select some common irregularly-spelt high frequency words, such as 'one', or 'would', and see how many of them the children can find in the text.

Vocabulary extension

- Brainstorm and list the sorts of characters one might find in fairy stories, such as prince, princess, wicked queen, fairy, dragon, giant. Do the same for places, such as castle, forest, cave, mountain.

ANSWERS

Thinking back

1 prince   2 princess   3 door   4 bed
5 mattresses   6 sleep   7 married

Thinking about it
(some suggested answers)
1 The prince wanted to marry a princess but he could not find one.
2 A princess was at the door.
3 Only a real princess would feel the pea under the mattresses.
4 The prince fell in love with the princess and they got married.

Thinking it through
1 unhappy   2 unhappy   3 unhappy
4 happy   5 happy   6 (open answer)

UNIT 8 The Princess and the Pea

Thinking back

Name _____   Date _____

Choose the correct word for each gap.

| door   mattresses   prince   bed   married   princess   sleep |

1 Once upon a time there lived a p_____ .

2 He wanted to marry a p_____ .

3 One night there was a knock at the d_____ .

4 The prince put a tiny pea on the b_____ .

5 On top of the pea he put twenty m_____ .

6 The princess could not s_____ very well.

7 The prince and the princess got m_____ .

Focus on Comprehension Teacher's Book 'A'. Text © Louis Fidge 1999
Illustrations © Nelson 1999. Published by Thomas Nelson and Sons Ltd 1999

Starter Book / Copymaster / Unit 8

UNIT 8 The Princess and the Pea   *Thinking about it*

Name _____   Date _____

Write the answers.

What was my problem at the beginning of the story?

1 _____
_____
_____

Who was at the door?

2 _____
_____

Why did I put a pea and twenty mattresses on the bed?

3 _____
_____
_____

How did the story end?

4 _____
_____
_____

UNIT 8 The Princess and the Pea   *Thinking it through*

Name _____   Date _____

Draw the best face.

1 How did the prince feel at the beginning of the story?

2 How did the princess feel when she was wet?

3 How did the princess feel in bed?

4 How did the prince feel when he found out the princess was a real princess?

5 How did the prince and princess feel when they got married?

6 Write something you liked about the story.

_____
_____
_____
_____

UNIT 9 Hoppers and Jumpers

Starter Book

FURTHER TEACHING OPPORTUNITIES

Text level

Reading comprehension
- Tell children the title of the unit and ask them what they think it is going to be about. Ask children to explain what insects are and to list as many as they are able.
- Explain that this unit is not a story (fiction) but gives information (non-fiction).
- Look at, and discuss, each picture one at a time and read the accompanying text to and with the children. Whilst doing so, reinforce that the information given is factual and true (whereas stories are imaginary).
- Explain that non-fiction books often contain pictures, and show how the captions relate to the pictures.
- If possible, have a simple reference book on insects available. Discuss the front and back covers, the book blurb and title, and acquaint children with some of the features of non-fiction books including contents and index pages.

Writing composition
- Ask children to draw a picture of one of the insects in the unit, and to write some questions about the insect under their pictures that are not answered in the unit. Discuss how they might find the answers.
- Encourage the children to write labels for diagrams, such as parts of their bodies.

Sentence level

Grammatical awareness
- Reproduce some of the sentences from the unit but leave out specific words such as the verbs as in 'A jumping spider _____ flies.' Ask children to fill in the missing words (using grammatical cues).

Sentence construction and punctuation
- Ask children to write three interesting facts they have discovered from the unit. Ensure that they punctuate each sentence correctly.

Word level

Phonics, word recognition and spelling
- 'Pla*nt*' contains a common final consonant blend. Think of other words ending in 'nt'. Do the same for 'ju*mp*', 'he*lp*' and 'lo*ng*'.
- There are many opportunities to study interesting features of different words such as looking for small words in longer words as in 'c*ats*'; finding words with double letters as in ho*pp*er; looking for long and short words; thinking of words made from two words as in 'grasshopper' and 'springtail'; looking for high frequency words.
- Use some words from the text to introduce the spelling of regular plurals such as one spider - two spiders; one leg - two legs; one tail - two tails. Extend this to other common nouns which may be pluralised by the addition of 's'.

Vocabulary extension
- Brainstorm and list as many insects as possible. (Link this to the opening suggestion in the comprehension section.)
- Use reference books on insects to help children draw and label parts of the bodies of different insects such as ants, butterflies.

ANSWERS

Thinking back
1 legs   2 cats and dogs   3 jumping spider
4 plants   5 tail

Thinking about it
Children have to label each picture correctly.

Thinking it through
Jumping spiders eat flies.   Dogs eat meat.
Rabbits eat carrots.   Sheep eat grass.
Birds eat worms.   Sharks eat fish.
(open answers) Children are asked to draw some of their favourite food.

UNIT 9 Hoppers and Jumpers

Thinking back

Name _____ Date _____

Finish the sentences.

A grasshopper has long back _____ .

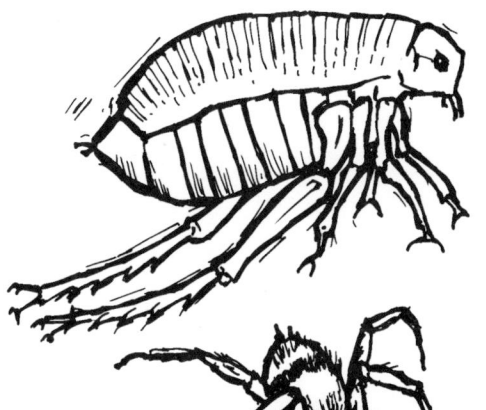

A flea jumps onto animals like _____ and _____ .

A _____ _____ eats flies.

Jumping plant lice live on _____ .

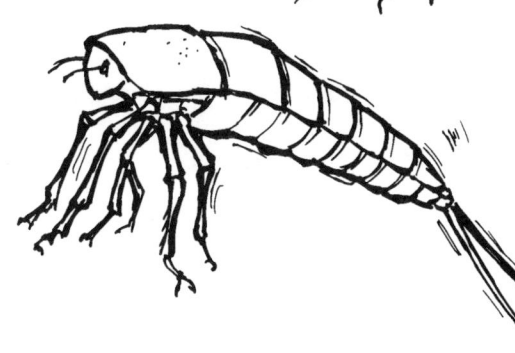

A springtail uses its _____ to help it jump.

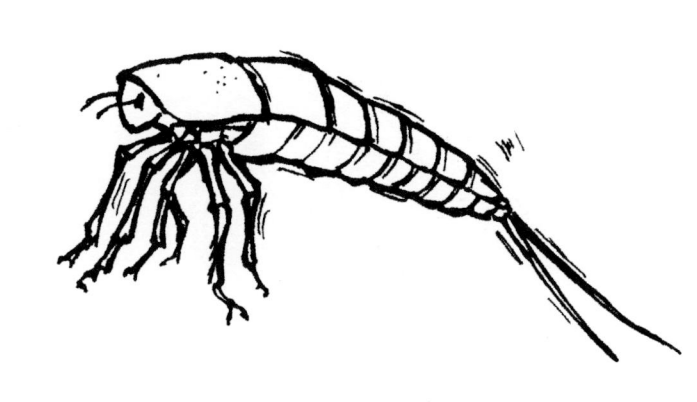

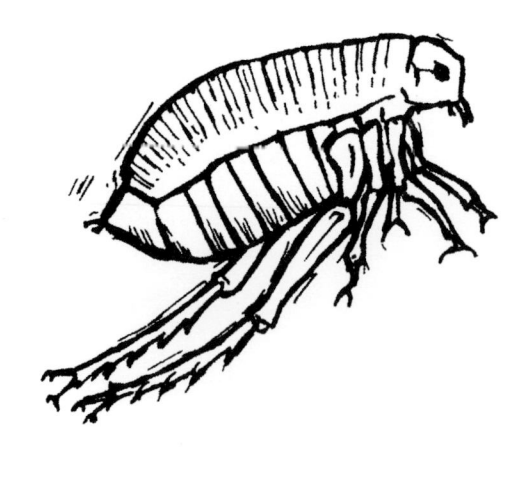

UNIT 9 Hoppers and Jumpers

Thinking about it

Name _____ Date _____

Label the pictures correctly.

| a grasshopper | a flea | a jumping spider |

| jumping plant lice | a springtail |

UNIT 9 Hoppers and Jumpers

Thinking it through

Name _____ Date _____

What do they eat?

Jumping spiders eat   carrots.

Dogs eat   worms.

Rabbits eat   flies.

Sheep eat   meat.

Birds eat   fish.

Sharks eat   grass.

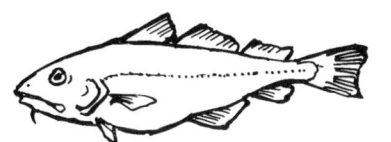

What do you like to eat? Draw and label some pictures of your favourite food.

Focus on Comprehension Teacher's Book 'A'. Text © Louis Fidge 1999
Illustrations © Nelson 1999. Published by Thomas Nelson and Sons Ltd 1999

Starter Book / Copymaster / Unit 9

UNIT 10 Rhymes from Around the World
Starter Book

FURTHER TEACHING OPPORTUNITIES

Text level

Reading comprehension
- Ask children to tell each other any rhymes they know. Explain that rhymes are popular with children all over the world.
- Look at where each of the rhymes come from in the unit and find these places on a globe if possible (assume the Muslim rhyme comes from the Middle East and the Gujarati rhyme from India).
- Read and discuss each rhyme one at a time. Encourage children to learn and recite the first two rhymes from memory.
- Explain any unfamiliar vocabulary, such as muezzin and mosque in rhyme three.
- Explain that the fourth rhyme is in fact a translation from another language.
- Ask children which rhyme they preferred. Encourage them to express their responses and personal views.

Writing composition
- The first two rhymes lend themselves well to use as models which can be adapted, experimenting with word substitution in places, allowing the children to make up their own rhymes. Additional verses could be made up and added to the originals.

Sentence level

Grammatical awareness
- The first rhyme is interesting in that it is written in parts in non-standard English. Children could be asked to identify any changes that could be made to it.
- Reproduce the third or fourth rhyme but leave out all the nouns. Ask children to supply the missing nouns.

Sentence construction and punctuation
- When reading the rhymes, draw attention to how the commas at the end of some lines signal the reader to make a pause.

Word level

Phonics, word recognition and spelling
- Use the following words from the rhymes to stimulate work on word endings, by suggesting and writing others with similar endings: ti*ll* and ba*ck*.
- Use some words from the text to stimulate work on the spelling of regular plurals. Extend this to other common nouns which may be pluralised by the addition of 's'.

Vocabulary extension
- Find and list the pairs of rhyming words from the rhymes. Ask children to suggest others in each family. Study and discuss the lists generated for common letter patterns and use opportunities for word-building.

ANSWERS

Thinking back
Children are asked to write out two rhymes correctly:
Pussy in de moonlight
Pussy in de zoo
Pussy never come home
Till half past two.

Charley over the water,
Charley over the sea,
Charley can catch a blackbird,
But he can't catch me!

Thinking about it
1. a) a cat (a pussy) b) a blackbird
   c) a pony d) a goat
2. at half past two
3. Charley is over the sea.
4. The pony went to the mosque.
5. (open answer)

Thinking it through
1. zoo – two   sea – me   anywhere – prayer
   go – snow   meet – eat   boo – too
2. (open answer)
3. bag – rag   ten – men   sun – fun
   sit – bit   top – shop   dress – mess
   sack – back

UNIT 10 Rhymes from Around the World

Thinking back

Name _____ Date _____

These two rhymes have got muddled up. Write each rhyme correctly.

Pussy in de moonlight

Charley over the sea,

Pussy never come home

But he can't catch me!

Charley over the water,

Pussy in de zoo

Charley can catch a blackbird,

Till half past two.

Rhyme 1 _____

Rhyme 2 _____

UNIT 10 Rhymes from Around the World

Thinking about it

Name _____ Date _____

Look at pupils' book, page 12.

1 What animal is mentioned in:

  a) rhyme **1**? _____

  b) rhyme **2**? _____

  c) rhyme **3**? _____

  d) rhyme **4**? _____

2 Read rhyme 1 again.
  What time did the pussy cat come home?

  _____

3 Read rhyme 2 again.
  Who is over the sea?

  _____

4 Read rhyme 3 again.
  Where did the little pony go?

  _____

5 Read rhyme 4 again.
  Why do you think the goat was crying?

  _____

UNIT 10 Rhymes from Around the World

Thinking it through

Name _____ Date _____

1 Look on page 12 of the pupils' book.
Find the word that rhymes with each of these:

zoo _____   sea _____

anywhere _____   go _____

meet _____   boo _____

2 Which rhyme on page 12 did you like best? Say why.

_____
_____
_____
_____
_____
_____

3 Match up the rhyming words.

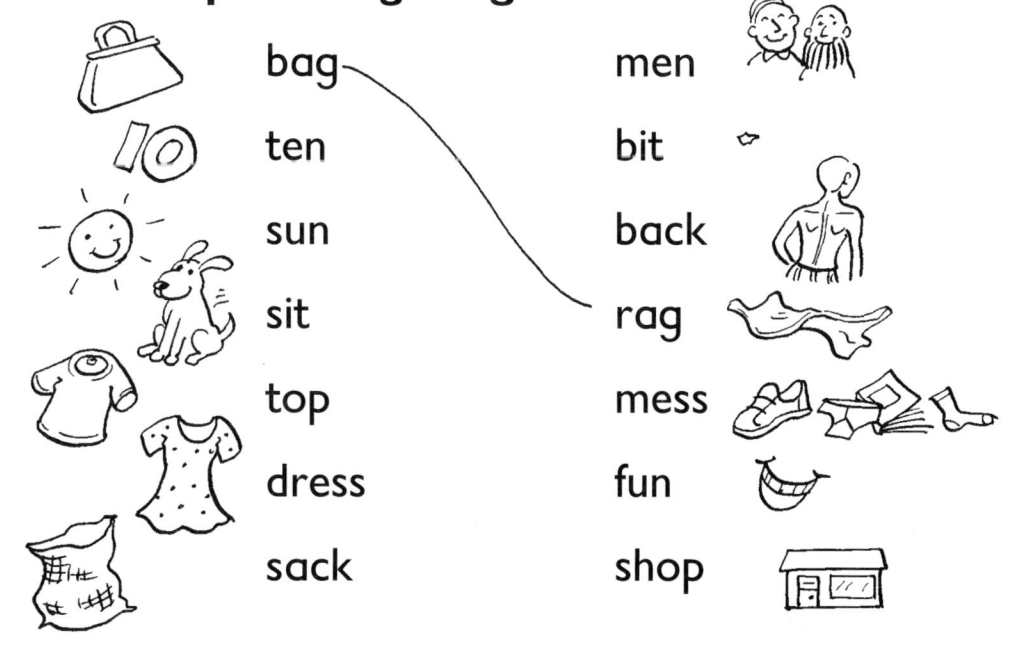

bag — rag

ten   men

sun   bit

sit   back

top   mess

dress   fun

sack   shop

UNIT 11 The Deaf Man and the Blind Man Starter Book

FURTHER TEACHING OPPORTUNITIES

Text level

Reading comprehension
- Read the title of the story. Ask children to suggest what some of the difficulties of being blind or deaf might be.
- Read the story to and with the children. During the reading, encourage the use of phonological, contextual, grammatical and graphic knowledge to work out, predict and check the meanings of unfamiliar words and to make sense of what is read.
- Discuss reasons why there might have been a lot of fighting in the town, and why the people of the town moved to another place.
- Ask the children what they thought of the townspeople for leaving the blind and deaf men.
- How did the two men resolve their difficulties? Ask the children why they think the king made the promise he did at the end of the story.
- Draw attention to the way the story begins and ends. Compare it with The Princess and the Pea. Both begin with the same words and begin with a problem of some sort. Both eventually turn out all right in the end.
- Ask the children to retell the story in their own words and then compare their version with the original. Are there any major differences?
- If appropriate find, read and discuss the story of Helen Keller or Louis Braille.

Writing composition
- Encourage children to suggest ways in which they can help others in everyday situations, such as at school, at home. List some suggestions. Ask children to draw some pictures illustrating some of these and to write simple captions for each picture.

Sentence level

Grammatical awareness
- Provide the children with some sentences from the text but with a word changed so it does not make sense in the context; for example, 'The deaf man could not see.' Ask them to spot the mistake.

Sentence construction and punctuation
- Provide the children with some short sentences based on the story to punctuate correctly, using capital letters at the beginning and full stops at the end of each.

Word level

Phonics, word recognition and spelling
- Use the word 'king' from the story. Ask children to suggest other 'ing' words and list them on the board for study. Do the same for 'ang', 'ong' and 'ung' words.
- Use the word 'blind' to focus on final consonant blends. Think of other words ending in 'and', 'end', 'ind', 'ond' and 'und' and practise making the words by blending the various phonemes. Extend this to other common final consonant blends.
- There are many regular and irregularly-spelt high frequency words in the text. Reproduce the text. Provide children with a list of high frequency words to focus on and get them to identify and circle all the words they can find in the text. Use these words as a basis for spelling practice.

Vocabulary extension
- Not all communication is verbal. Discuss how body language and gestures can communicate meaning. Draw some examples of facial expressions and the use of hands to communicate meaning. Under each write and say what they mean.

ANSWERS

Thinking back
1 blind   2 deaf   3 see   4 hear
5 town   6 friend   7 again

Thinking about it
1 because there was a lot of fighting.
2 (open answer)   3 (open answer)   4 (open answer)

Thinking it through
(open answers)
The children have to draw and label some things they would miss most if they could not see or hear.

UNIT 11 The Deaf Man and the Blind Man

Thinking back

Name _____ Date _____

Choose the best word to finish each sentence.

1 One man was _____ .   (blind, wet)

2 One man was _____ .   (hot, deaf)

3 The blind man could not _____ .   (see, hear)

4 The deaf man could not _____ .   (see, hear)

5 The people moved to another _____ .   (farm, town)

6 The deaf man helped his _____ .   (friend, king)

7 The king promised they would never be left _____ .
   (always, again)

UNIT 11 The Deaf Man and the Blind Man

Thinking about it

Name _____   Date _____

Write the answers to these questions.

1 Why did the people leave the town?

   The people left the town because _____

   _____

2 Do you think it was kind to leave the blind man and the deaf man behind?

   I do not think it was kind to leave them behind because

   _____

   _____

3 How do you think the blind man and the deaf man helped each other?

   I think _____

   _____

4 What do you think the king said when he saw the two men?

Starter Book / Copymaster / Unit 11

UNIT 11 The Deaf Man and the Blind Man

Thinking it through

Name _____ Date _____

Draw and label some of the things you would miss most if you couldn't hear.

Draw and label some of the things you would miss most if you couldn't see.

UNIT 12 An ABC of People

Starter Book

FURTHER TEACHING OPPORTUNITIES

Text level

Reading comprehension

- Begin by revising children's knowledge of the alphabet. Discuss the fact that just as the letters of the alphabet are in a particular order, so some books are arranged in alphabetical order. If children have word books refer to these. Show them the class register. Have a picture or a simple dictionary available to show them.
- Read each entry one at a time. Point out that each entry begins with the first letter of the person in a picture (how helpful is this?), the name of the job the person does and a definition (a sentence giving the meaning of the word, in this case, explaining what the person does).
- Try to think of other jobs beginning with each letter.
- Encourage children to refer to, and use, other simple picture dictionaries.

Writing composition

- Together, compose and write some other sentences about each job mentioned in the unit.
- Try to think of other jobs for each letter of the alphabet and make a class Alphabet of People.

Sentence level

Grammatical awareness

- Mix up the beginnings and endings of each definition, such as 'An astronaut makes bread and cakes', and ask children to explain what is wrong with each.

Sentence construction and punctuation

- This unit is ideal for discussing and identifying sentences as it contains both single word captions and sentences.

Word level

Phonics, word recognition and spelling

- Use the words 'tri*ck*' and 'thi*ng*' to stimulate work on the 'ck' and 'ng' ending. Think of other words phonically regular, monosyllabic words ending with these sounds.
- The words '*sp*ace', '*br*ead', '*cl*own', '*tr*icks', '*gr*ows' all begin with common consonant clusters. Think of, and list, other words beginning with the same clusters. Make up sentences containing the new words listed.

Vocabulary extension

- Much of the work suggested above concerns vocabulary development. Further work could be done on each person, however. Simple pictures involving labels and captions could be made for each; for example, what an astronaut wears; jobs a farmer does, and so on.

ANSWERS

Thinking back

Children have to arrange pictures of astronaut, baker, clown, dentist, electrician and farmer in alphabetical order.

Thinking about it

astronaut – someone who goes into space in a spaceship
baker – someone who makes bread and cakes
clown – someone who does tricks and makes us laugh
dentist – someone who looks after our teeth
electrician – someone who repairs electrical things
farmer – someone who works on a farm

Thinking it through

librarian – someone who looks after books in a library
musician – someone who plays a musical instrument
nurse – someone who looks after the sick
optician – someone who looks after our eyes
pilot – someone who flies an aeroplane
queen – someone who is head of a country

UNIT 12 An ABC of People

Thinking back

Name _____ Date _____

Cut out the pictures.
Arrange them in alphabetical order.

| dentist |  astronaut |  electrician |
|  clown |  farmer |  baker |

UNIT 12 An ABC of People

Thinking about it

Name _____   Date _____

Match up each person with the correct sentence.

astronaut	Someone who does tricks and makes us laugh.
baker	Someone who works on a farm.
clown	Someone who goes into space in a spaceship.
dentist	Someone who repairs electrical things.
electrician	Someone who makes bread and cakes.
farmer	Someone who looks after our teeth.

UNIT 12 An ABC of People

Thinking it through

Name _____   Date _____

Write the correct sentence next to each picture.

| Someone who flies an aeroplane. |
| Someone who looks after the sick. |
| Someone who is head of a country. |
| Someone who looks after books in a library. |
| Someone who looks after our eyes. |
| Someone who plays a musical instrument. |

librarian _____

musician _____

nurse _____

optician _____

pilot _____

queen _____

UNIT 13 King Rollo and the New Shoes — Starter Book

FURTHER TEACHING OPPORTUNITIES

Text level

Reading comprehension
- Introduce the unit by discussing the sorts of shoes children prefer.
- Discuss the difficulties of tying up laces or ties. This could be linked to a discussion on the satisfaction of mastering any difficult skill (like reading or writing!)
- Read the title and the introductory paragraph together. If possible, mask the text under each picture. Study and discuss the sequence of pictures. What can be learnt from them? How much sense do they make on their own?
- Next read the caption under each picture, drawing attention to the help each picture gives in aiding the meaning.
- Ask questions to check the literal understanding of the text; for example, What was the name of the king? the queen?. Ask questions prompting children to think about the causes of things, such as Why did the king visit the shoe shop? Why was there a crash? Ask more probing questions, such as Why do you think the magician didn't cast a spell to do up the king's shoe laces?
- If appropriate, consider other stories such as fairy stories, containing kings, queens, magicians.

Writing composition
- Ask children to identify the main characters in the story and to comment on their appearance, behaviour and qualities. Together, write a character profile of one of them.
- Encourage children to retell the story in their own words. Draw pictures and help children write simple sentence captions under each. Compare their versions with the original.

Sentence level

Grammatical awareness
- Reproduce some of the sentences from the text, leaving a word out from each for the children to fill in. If the same type of word is omitted each time such as a noun or preposition, then this helps focus on the grammatical functions these words perform.

Sentence construction and punctuation
- Children often think a line of writing is the same as a sentence. Use the captions under the pictures to help dispel this notion.
- Notice how dialogue is presented, both in speech bubbles in the pictures and in speech marks in the text.
- Notice, too, how capital letters are sometimes used for emphasis (as in the word CRASH).

Word level

Phonics, word recognition and spelling
- Focus on initial letter sounds of words by experimentation: for example, take a simple word from the text like 'went'. Change the first letter to 'b', 's', 't'. What new words can be made? Do the same with final letters: for instance, change the 'final 'd' of 'did' to 'g', 'm', 'p'.
- Have fun with alliteration (King Rollo likes rocks, reindeer, robins, rooks, ravioli and robots). Link this to children's own names.
- Have a 'high frequency word hunt'. Provide children with a hit list of high frequency words and ask them to see how many they can find in the text.

Vocabulary extension
- How many different types of footwear can the children come up with?

ANSWERS

Thinking back
1 King Rollo 2 the magician 3 Queen Gwen
4 the cook   5 King Rollo

Thinking about it
1 (False)   2 (True)   3 (True)
4 (False)   5 (True)   6 (True)
7 (False)   8 (True)

Thinking it through
(open answer)

UNIT 13 King Rollo and the New Shoes

Thinking back

Name _____   Date _____

1 Write the correct name under each picture.

| magician | cook | King Rollo | Queen Gwen |

_____ _____ _____ _____

Write the answers.

2 Who got some new shoes?

_____

3 Who showed the king how to do his shoes up?

_____

4 Who came to have tea with King Rollo?

_____

5 Who took Queen Gwen to the king's room?

_____

6 Who did up his own shoe laces?

_____

UNIT 13 King Rollo and the New Shoes

Thinking about it

Name _____ Date _____

Say if each sentence is true (T) or false (F).

1 King Rollo had a shoe shop. _____

2 King Rollo got some new shoes. _____

3 The king's shoes had laces. _____

4 The queen showed the king how to do up his shoes. _____

5 King Rollo went into his room to practise doing up his laces. _____

6 Queen Gwen came to have tea with King Rollo. _____

7 The magician took the queen to King Rollo's room. _____

8 The queen liked the king's new shoes. _____

UNIT 13 King Rollo and the New Shoes

Thinking it through

Name _____ Date _____

Tick ✓ the things you can do.

Cross ✗ the things you can't do.

tie your laces ☐	click your fingers ☐	play the piano ☐
swim ☐	wink ☐	knit ☐
thread a needle ☐	stand on your head ☐	kiss a spider ☐

Write some things that are too hard for you to do yet.

UNIT 14 Birds in the Rainforest

Starter Book

FURTHER TEACHING OPPORTUNITIES

Text level

Reading comprehension
- Before reading the text ask children to volunteer anything they know about rainforests.
- Explain that this unit is not a story (fiction) but gives information (non-fiction).
- Look at, and discuss, each picture one at a time and read the accompanying text to and with the children. Whilst doing so, reinforce that the information given is factual and true (whereas stories are imaginary).
- Explain that non-fiction books often contain pictures, and show how the captions relate to the pictures.
- If possible, have a simple reference book on rain forests available. Discuss the front and back covers, the book blurb and title, and acquaint children with some of the features of non-fiction books including contents and index pages.

Writing composition
- Ask children to draw a picture of one of the birds mentioned in the unit and write some questions about the animal under their pictures that are not answered in the unit. Discuss how they might find the answers.
- Encourage the children to draw a picture of a tree showing all the various birds mentioned in it. Get them to write labels for each bird.

Sentence level

Grammatical awareness
- Reproduce some of the sentences from the text and ask children to suggest alternative words as substitutes for some words, which will not affect the meaning at all; for example, 'Lots of (many) birds (insects, animals) live (may be found, stay) in the trees (bushes) in the rainforest (jungle).'

Sentence construction and punctuation
- Ask children to draw a picture of one of the animals mentioned and to write a couple of facts they found interesting under it, ensuring that they punctuate each sentence correctly.

Word level

Phonics, word recognition and spelling
- The following words from the text begin with different consonant blends: '*tr*ee, *cr*ack, *sm*all'. Ask children to suggest other words beginning with the same sounds. Encourage children to make up sentences containing the suggested words.
- Use the word 'tree' to introduce the long 'ee' sound. Make the words 'bee', 'free', 'see', 'three' by analogy. Use the word 'eat' to introduce the 'ea' sound, noticing how it sound similar to the 'ee' phoneme. Make the words 'beat', 'heat', 'meat', 'seat', 'treat' by analogy.

Vocabulary extension
- Discuss vocabulary related to trees such as 'trunk', 'branch', 'bark', 'root', 'leaf'.

ANSWERS

Thinking back
1 birds	2 beak	3 colourful
4 small	5 bird of paradise	6 leaves

Thinking about it
Birds that live in the rainforest:
   toucan, parrot, hummingbird, hoatzin, bird of paradise
Animals that live in the sea:
   shark, whale, fish, octopus, dolphin

Thinking it through
	Picture number
a parrot	3
a hoatzin	6
a toucan	2
a bird of paradise	5
a hummingbird	4
(open answers)	

UNIT 14 Birds in the Rainforest   Thinking back

Name _____   Date _____

Find the answers on page 16 in your book.
Fill in the missing words.

1 Lots of _____ live in the trees in the rainforest.

2 A toucan has a big _____ .

3 A parrot has _____ feathers.

4 A hummingbird is very _____ .

5 A _____ of _____ has long feathers.

6 A hoatzin eats _____ .

UNIT 14 Birds in the Rainforest

Thinking about it

Name _____   Date _____

Write the name of each animal in the chart in the correct place.

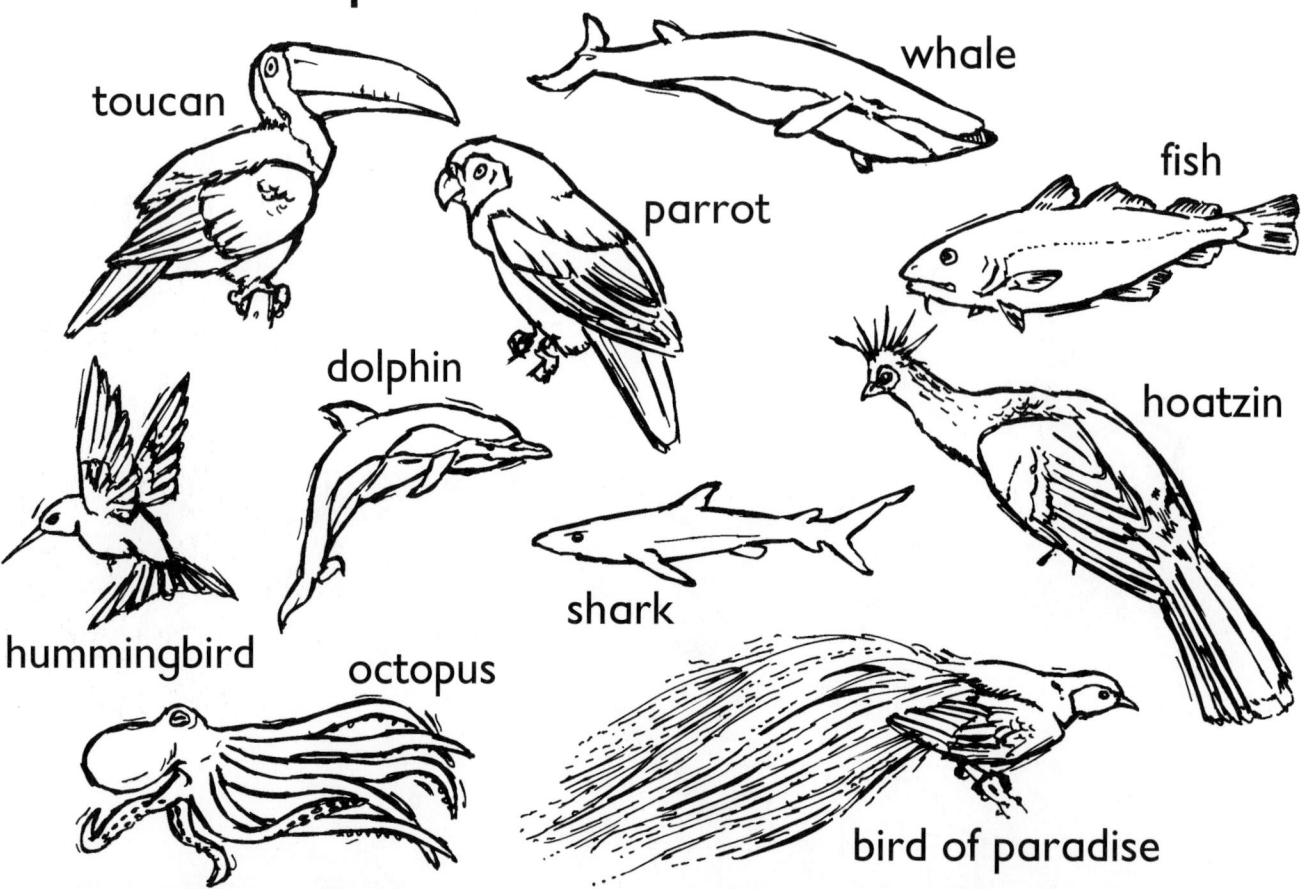

toucan
whale
parrot
fish
dolphin
hoatzin
hummingbird
shark
octopus
bird of paradise

Birds that live in the rainforest	Animals that live in the sea

UNIT 14 Birds in the Rainforest — Thinking it through

Name _____ Date _____

On page 16 of your book, you can find information on each of the following birds. Write the correct picture number in the chart below.

name	picture number
a parrot	3
a hoatzin	
a toucan	
a bird of paradise	
a hummingbird	

Write three facts from page 16 that you found very interesting.

_____

_____

_____

_____

_____

UNIT 15 Wind on the Hill

Starter Book

FURTHER TEACHING OPPORTUNITIES

Text level

Reading comprehension
- Encourage children to share their anecdotal experiences of flying kites.
- Look together at the title and picture on the page and ask children to suggest what they think the unit is going to be about.
- Explain that this is a fiction text (it is not necessarily true) and is a poem. Note the way it is set out in verses, and look at the name of the poet. Have the children read any stories or poems by the same author?
- Read the poem, to and with the children, several times, emphasising the rhyming elements. Encourage the children to join in when they feel confident.
- Ask children for their personal responses to the poem. What did they like (or not like) about it?
- If possible read and compare other poems about the wind. (The poem on the 'Think it through' copymaster is good for this purpose.) Collect some of the children's favourite weather poems as a class anthology and use them for practice in reading aloud.

Writing composition
- As a class, compile a list poem, beginning each line with 'The wind is …' Explain that list poems do not have to rhyme.

Sentence level

Grammatical awareness
- Encourage children to read the poem, as it becomes familiar, with pace and expression appropriate to the grammar; for example, pausing at full stops and commas, using appropriate expression.
- Reproduce a verse from the poem with the lines in the wrong order. Ask children to resequence the lines so they make sense.

Sentence construction and punctuation
- Encourage the children to make up questions about the weather that they would like to know the answers to (for instance, Where does the wind come from? Why can't you see the wind?) Draw attention to the need for question marks at the end of questions.

Word level

Phonics, word recognition and spelling
- Identify the pairs of rhyming words in the poem. Which pairs contain the same letter patterns (for instance, 'ran' and 'can')? Which contain different letter patterns ('knows' and 'goes'). Brainstorm and list other words that rhyme with the identified words and sort according to common letter patterns.
- Use the work on rhyming words to focus on the 'oo' phoneme (as exemplified by the word 'too'). Use this as an opportunity for generating, studying and discussing words containing the phonemes: 'oo' (as in moon); 'u-e' as in (tune); 'ew' (as in flew); 'ue' (as in blue).

Vocabulary extension
- Ask children to suggest the ways in which wind is helpful and contrast this with the damage winds can do.
- Brainstorm describing words and phrases about different types of winds; for example, gentle soft summer breezes; howling gales.

ANSWERS

Thinking back
Children are asked to arrange the verses of the poem in order as per the unit.

Thinking about it
1. knows – goes   can – ran
   kite – night   goes knows
2. (open answer)
3. I like to ride my bike.
   A kite can fly up in the sky.
   I like to play on a sunny day.
   There was a frog sitting on a log (dog, bog).
   You can go far in a car (star).

Thinking it through
(open answer)

UNIT 15 Wind on the Hill

Thinking back

Name _____ Date _____

**The verses of the poem are in the wrong order.
Cut them out and arrange them correctly.
When you have finished, read the poem to a friend.**

No one can tell me,
Nobody knows,
Where the wind comes from,
Where the wind goes.

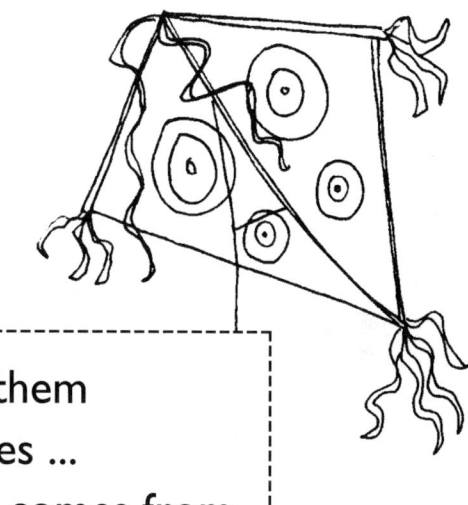

So then I could tell them
Where the wind goes ...
But where the wind comes from
Nobody knows.

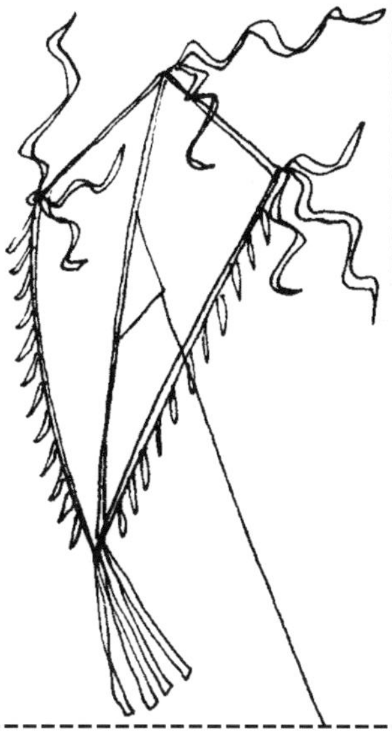

But if I stopped holding
The string on my kite,
It would blow with the wind
For a day and a night.

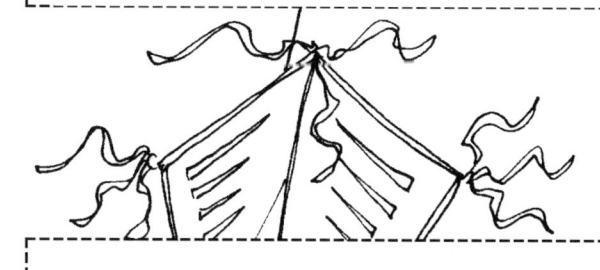

It's flying from somewhere
As fast as it can,
I couldn't keep up with it,
Not if I ran.

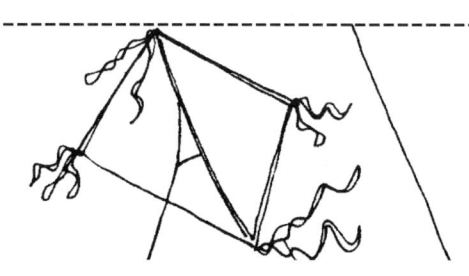

And then when I found it,
Wherever it blew,
I should know that the wind
Had been going there too.

UNIT 15 Wind on the Hill

Thinking about it

Name _____   Date _____

1 Write a word from the poem on pupils' book page 17 that rhymes with each word in the kites.

kites: knows, can, blow, kite

2 Now think of some more rhyming words for each kite.

3 Think of a rhyming word to go with the underlined word, and complete each sentence.

I <u>like</u> to ride my _____ .

A kite can <u>fly</u> up in the _____ .

I like to <u>play</u> on a sunny _____ .

There was a <u>frog</u> sitting on a _____ .

You can go <u>far</u> in a _____ .

Starter Book / Copymaster / Unit 15

UNIT 15 Wind on the Hill

Thinking it through

Name _____ Date _____

**Practise reading this poem about the wind.
Read the poem to a friend.**

Wind

The wind blows the windmill,
the wind blows me.
Where does the wind go?
Can you see?

The wind blows feathers,
the wind blows fluff,
whirling around
all kinds of stuff.

Paper, flags,
and leaves and hair –
what do they do
when the wind's not there?

The wind blows the sea
with a splosh and a splash;
the wind blows the window –
bang and crash!

The wind blows around
like a roundabout.
Hold on tightly
or he'll blow you out!

**Which poem about the wind did you like best –
the poem on pupils' book page 17 or this poem? Why?**

_____

_____

_____

UNIT 16 Crow's Problem

Starter Book

FURTHER TEACHING OPPORTUNITIES

Text level

Reading comprehension
- This story is interesting in that it is both a story and can be used as an information text (demonstrating the displacement of water).
- The story is all about solving a tricky problem. Introduce the unit by asking some questions like 'What would you do if... (you got locked out; you got your head stuck in some railings)?' encouraging divergent responses.
- Look at each picture and read each caption one at a time. Discuss each picture prior to reading the caption to help contextualise the text.
- After reading the first picture and text, discuss what the initial problem is and ask children for their ideas on how they might solve it.
- Ask the children what they thought of Crow. Why was his solution such a good idea? Discuss why his solution worked. (If possible, try it out in class!)
- Why do the children think Crow was so thirsty to begin with?
- After reading the story ask children for their personal responses to the story.

Writing composition
- Ask children to retell the story in sequence, using words like first, next, after, when. Help them to write up a recount using simple sentences.
- Carry out a simple experiment to find which things float and which things sink in water and ask the children to recount what happened.

Sentence level

Grammatical awareness
- The story lends itself to being read aloud. Encourage children to read the story with pace and expression appropriate to the grammar and meaning.
- Use the sentences from the recount produced in the writing composition section. Cut them up and ask children to sequence them correctly, paying attention to key words such as 'first', 'next'.

Sentence construction and punctuation
- Draw attention to the purpose of full stops by reading the text aloud to the children, ignoring the full stops (as though it is one continuous flow). Ask children what they noticed and how it affected their ability to understand.

Word level

Phonics, word recognition and spelling
- Use the word 'day' from the text. Ask children to suggest other 'ay' words, including the days of the week. (Note that the 'ay' invariably comes at the end of each word.) Next introduce the word 'rain' and note how the 'ai' phoneme sounds the same as the 'ay' phoneme. By analogy work out other 'ain' words. (If appropriate provide some other words containing 'ai' such as 'wait', 'laid', 'mail'.) Note that 'ai' usually comes inside the words. If appropriate introduce the word 'tape' and note the sound of 'a-e' words. Try making some 'ade', 'ale', 'ame', 'ape', 'ate' words.
- Make a fishing rod with a ruler, a piece of string and a magnet. Make some key word cards and put a paperclip on each. Get the children to 'fish' for the cards. Those they know and can spell they keep. Who can collect most cards?

Vocabulary extension
- Write each letter of the alphabet on a separate card. Tape a metal clip to the back of the word cards with vowels on them. Ask children to discover which letters are magnetic. Allow this to lead into a discussion on vowels and consonants.

ANSWERS

Thinking back

1 hot	2 thirsty	3 jar	4 beak
5 stones	6 water	7 top	8 drink

Thinking about it
Children have to arrange pictures to tell the story and to write their own sentence to go with each picture.

Thinking it through
(open answers) Children have to carry out an experiment and write a report of their findings.

UNIT 16 Crow's Problem

Thinking back

Name _____ Date _____

Choose the correct word for each gap in the sentences below.

1 It was a _____ day. (hot/cold)

2 Crow was _____ . (hungry/thirsty)

3 Crow saw some water in a _____ . (jar/cup)

4 Crow was not able to reach the water with his _____ . (beak/claws)

5 Crow saw some _____ . (rocks/stones)

6 Crow dropped the stones in the _____ . (pond/water)

7 The stones made the water level rise to the _____ of the jar. (top/bottom)

8 Crow had a lovely _____ . (drink/meal)

UNIT 16 Crow's Problem

Thinking about it

Name _____ Date _____

Cut out the pictures.
Arrange them so they tell the story.
Make up a sentence to go with each picture.

Starter Book / Copymaster / Unit 16

UNIT 16 Crow's Problem

Thinking it through

Name _____ Date _____

In the story Crow carried out a simple experiment. Carry out this experiment and fill in what you discover.

You will need:

a magnet   a button   a pin   some paper   some string   a key

What to do:

Use the magnet. See which things it attracts and which things it does not attract.

Write down what you discover:

First I tried the _____ .

It _____ (was/was not) attracted to the magnet.

Next I tried the _____ .

It _____ (was/was not) attracted to the magnet.

After this _____

_____ .

Then _____

_____ .

Last of all, _____

_____ .

UNIT 17 Row Your Boat

Starter Book

FURTHER TEACHING OPPORTUNITIES

Text level

Reading comprehension
- Introduce this unit by singing and miming the traditional version of the rhyme: 'Row, row, row your boat, Gently down the stream. Merrily, merrily, merrily, Life is but a dream.' Explain that this unit plays about with the words of the rhyme.
- Look at, and discuss each picture. Ask children what they think the verse is going to be about prior to reading the accompanying verse.
- Ask children where each verse takes place. What animals are mentioned in the verses?
- Ask children what they would do if they meet each animal.
- Did the children like the poem? Ask for their opinions.
- Look at, and discuss, the way the poem is structured (four verses, with four lines in each verse). Draw attention to the patterned and predictable language structures used in the poem. Point out the name of the poet.
- Find, read and compare other humorous poems or poems with predictable and patterned language (for example, 'The wheels on the bus go round and round'). Encourage children to read them aloud once they become familiar. Collect together a number for a class anthology of favourites.

Writing composition
- Use the poem structure as a model. Encourage the children to substitute a different animal in each verse. This idea could be extended and the third and fourth lines of each verse could be substituted. (The 'Think it through' copymaster extends the idea even further.)

Sentence level

Grammatical awareness
- The first idea in the 'writing composition' section encourages the grammatical awareness of nouns.
- The verses could be reproduced with the verbs omitted. Ask children to suggest a suitable verb to go in each gap. (The verbs need not be the same as in the original.)

Sentence construction and punctuation
- Ask children to frame one or two questions of their own about each verse and to use question marks appropriately; for example, 'What do you row?'

Word level

Phonics, word recognition and spelling
- Use the word 'boat' from the text. Ask children to suggest other 'oat' words. Provide the children with other 'oa' words; for example, soap, toad, loaf, goal. (Note that 'oa' usually comes within the word.) Next introduce the word 'row' from the text and note how the 'ow' phoneme sometimes sounds the same as the 'oa' phoneme. By analogy work out other 'ow' words; for example, bow, low, mow, tow, grow, throw, know, blow, glow. Note that 'ow' often comes at the ends of words. If appropriate introduce the word 'home' from the text and note the sound of 'o-e' words. Try making some 'obe', 'ole', 'ome', 'one', 'ope' words.
- Use the verb 'watch' from the text. Notice how it can have 'ing' added; for example, 'I am watching' or 'ed' as in 'I watched'. Provide some other regular verbs and suffix them with 'ing' and 'ed', for example, call, jump, shiver, row, walk, shout. Look for other 'ing' and 'ed' words in books.

Vocabulary extension
- Take some key words from the text. Ask children to circle all the vowels in them. Discuss whether all words need vowels in them.

ANSWERS

Thinking back
1 Wave your arms and scream.
2 Watch out for the crocodile and look out for the snake.
3 Don't forget to shiver.
4 Ask her home for tea.

Thinking about it
(open answer) Children have to think of suitable rhyming words to go with stimulus words.

Thinking it through
(open answer) Children have to make up their own poem based on the one in the unit.

UNIT 17 Row Your Boat — Thinking back

Name _____   Date _____

1 What should you do if you catch a jellyfish?

_____

2 What should you watch out for on the lake?

_____

3 What shouldn't you forget to do if you see a polar bear?

_____

4 What should you do if you meet a big blue whale?

_____

UNIT 17 Row Your Boat

Thinking about it

Name _____ Date _____

1 Write a word on each ladder from the poem on pupils' books page 19 that rhymes with the following words:

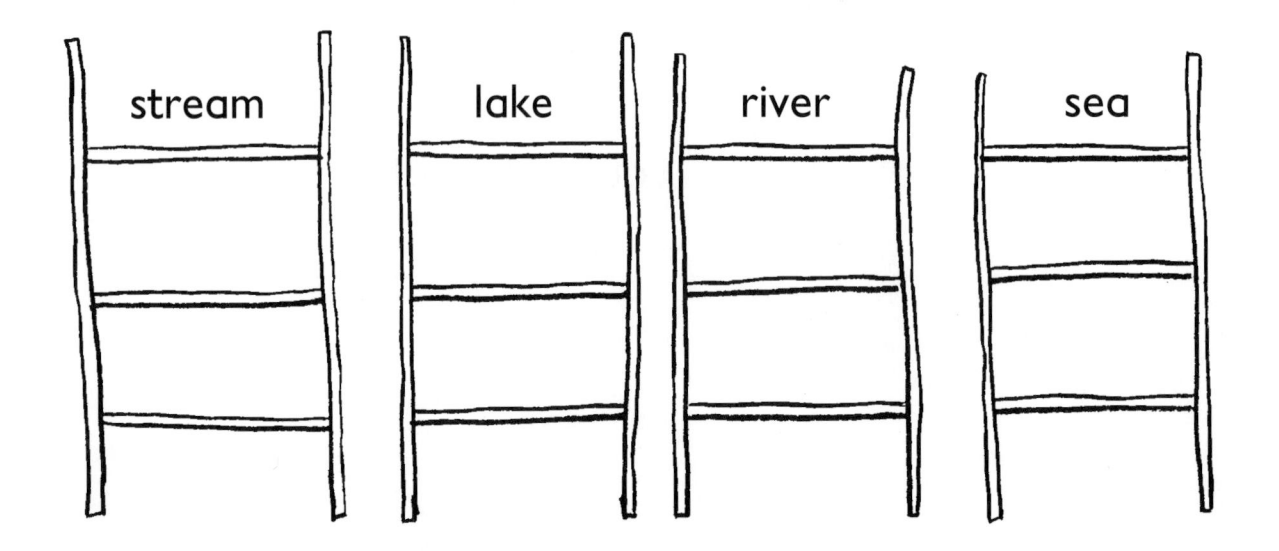

stream   lake   river   sea

2 Now think of one more rhyming word for each ladder.

3 Think of a rhyming word to go with the underlined word, and complete each sentence.

The <u>crocodile</u> has a lovely _____ .

The big blue <u>whale</u> has a long, long _____ .

The hissing <u>snake</u> was eating a _____ .

The <u>jellyfish</u> drank from a _____ .

The polar <u>bear</u> had long pink _____ .

UNIT 17 **Row Your Boat** Thinking it through

Name _____ Date _____

> Make up your own poem like the one on pupils' book page 19. Think of a way to finish each verse. Here is a verse I wrote to start you off.

Ride, ride, ride your bike
Gently down the road,
If you meet a big green frog
Pretend it is a toad.

Ride, ride, ride your bike
Gently down the street,

_____

_____ .

Ride, ride, ride your bike
Gently down the path,

_____

_____ .

Ride, ride, ride your bike
Gently down the lane,

_____

_____ .

UNIT 18 My Pet Hamster

Starter Book

FURTHER TEACHING OPPORTUNITIES

Text level

Reading comprehension
- Introduce the unit by doing a survey of what pets children in the class have. Follow this by a discussion of what each pet needs in order to be looked after properly. Ask children to recount any funny things that have happened with their pets.
- Look at the title and ask children to suggest what the story might be about.
- Look at, read and discuss each picture and caption one at a time. Notice how the pictures aid the reading of the text and how the text uses predictable and patterned language. Encourage the children to use pictures to help them when reading.
- What is the purpose of a cage? Ask children to suggest what it is made of.
- How do we know what food the hamster needed?
- Discuss some possible names for the hamster. List them. Can the children find lists of things around the classroom? What are they for?

Writing composition
- Ask children to retell the events in sequence, using words like 'first', 'next', 'after', 'when'. Help them to write up a recount using simple sentences.
- Encourage children to use labels such as to describe what a hamster (cat/ dog/ rabbit) needs.
- Make lists such as 'units I have completed/ people on my table/ food a rabbit needs'.

Sentence level

Grammatical awareness
- The text lends itself to being read aloud. Encourage children to read the story with pace and expression appropriate to the grammar, meaning and punctuation.
- Use the sentences from the recount produced in the writing composition section. Cut them up and ask children to sequence them correctly, paying attention to key words such as 'first', 'next'.

Sentence construction and punctuation
- Ask children to suggest names for the hamster, remembering to begin each with a capital letter. Extend this to work on the use of capitalisation for book titles and headings and for emphasis.

Word level

Phonics, word recognition and spelling
- Use the text for a 'phoneme hunt'. Look for words containing 'ee'; 'ay'; 'age'; 'ame'; 'oo'. Use the words found as a basis for further work on each phoneme.
- Use the verb 'need' from the text. Notice how it can have 'ing' added (needing) or 'ed' as in 'I needed'. Provide some other regular verbs and suffix them with 'ing' and 'ed'.

Vocabulary extension
- Find a reference book on pets. Look at and discuss the title, cover, blurb and use the contents and index pages to find information on specific pets. Compare how the information is presented in the book and in the unit. Make lists of essential things different animals need.

ANSWERS

Thinking back
1 cage   2 food   3 water
4 toy   5 naughty

Thinking about it
1 pet hamster   2 cage   3 toy
4 food   5 water   6 naughty!

Thinking it through
Things for a hamster:
  a cage, water, carrots, straw,
Things for a dog:
  a bone, a brush, a lead, a basket
Things for a budgie:
  a birdcage, bird food, a ladder, a mirror
Things for a goldfish:
  bowl, fish food, stones, weeds

UNIT 18 My Pet Hamster   Thinking back

Name _____   Date _____

**Look for the answers on page 20 of your book.
Finish each sentence.**

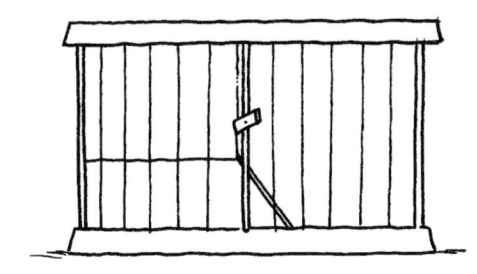

A hamster needs a _____ .

A hamster needs _____ .

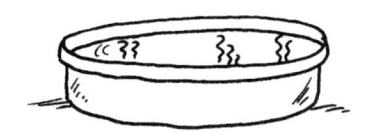

A hamster needs _____ .

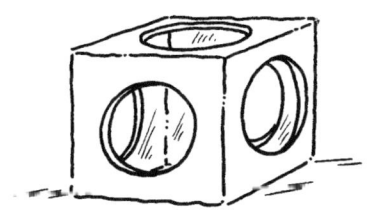

A hamster needs a _____ .

This hamster is being _____ !

UNIT 18 My Pet Hamster

Thinking about it

Name _____ Date _____

> What did I do for my hamster?
> Think of a way to finish each sentence below.
> Look for the answers on page 20 in your book.

1 First I got a _____ for my birthday.

2 Next I got a _____.

3 Then I got my hamster a _____.

4 After this I got my hamster some _____.

5 Then I got my hamster some _____.

6 Then my hamster was _____!

UNIT 18 My Pet Hamster

Thinking it through

Name _____ Date _____

**Decide what each pet would need.
Make a list for each pet.**

- a bone
- fish food
- carrots
- a bird cage
- a hamster cage
- a basket
- straw
- a lead
- a brush
- bird food
- a mirror
- water
- a bowl
- stones and weeds
- a ladder

Things for a hamster	Things for a dog
_____	_____
_____	_____
_____	_____
_____	_____

Things for a budgie	Things for a goldfish
_____	_____
_____	_____
_____	_____
_____	_____

UNIT 19 Ready for Winter

Starter Book

FURTHER TEACHING OPPORTUNITIES

Text level

Reading comprehension
- Introduce the unit with a quotation from Frog from the story. 'Winter is beautiful,' he said. Do children agree or disagree? What do they associate winter with?
- Look at the title – what things have to be done to get ready for winter?
- The unit is divided into three sections. Look at the picture, read and discuss the text for each section one at a time.
- After the first section ask how Frog and Toad each perceive winter. Is Toad happy at being woken by Frog? Why not?
- After reading the middle section ask if Frog was put off by Toad's moans. How had Frog come prepared? How did Frog get Toad ready for winter?
- Read the last section and ask children what Toad thought of the sledge. Why might Toad have been frightened?
- Where did the story take place? Do animals really talk to each other?
- Read the poem from the 'Think it through' copymaster and compare it with the story.

Writing composition
- Provide children with a series of three empty frames and ask them to draw three things that happened in the story. Under each frame get them to write a simple sentence.
- Ask children what they think happened next. Encourage them to draw a picture and to write some simple sentences under it. (Use the 'Think about it' copymaster if appropriate.)

Sentence level

Grammatical awareness
- Reread the text with the children. Select appropriate words from it and ask them to suggest alternatives, such as: 'Winter is _____ lovely, nice, cold, exciting,' said Frog.

Sentence construction and punctuation
- Provide children with a few simple questions based on the text. Ask them to punctuate each question correctly, using a capital to begin with and for proper nouns and finishing each sentence with a question mark.

Word level

Phonics, word recognition and spelling
- Use the word 'my' from the text. Replace the 'm' with 'b', 'cr', 'sk', 'fl', 'tr', 'sl'. Discuss the new words made. Use this to lead into work on other similar sounding phonemes, such as 'igh' (as in high, sigh, light, might, tight, night); 'ie' (as in lie, pie, die); 'i-e' words containing 'ide', 'ife', 'ike', 'ile', 'ime', 'ine', 'ipe', 'ite'.
- Have a 'high frequency word hunt', including both regular and irregular words. Provide children with a hit list of high frequency words and ask them to see how many they can find in the text.

Vocabulary extension
- Ask children to compare and contrast summer and winter using certain variables, such as clothes worn, weather, games played, preferred food and drink.

ANSWERS

Thinking back
1 Frog   2 Toad   3 Toad
4 Frog   5 Frog   6 Frog

Thinking about it
1 He called to ask him to come out to play.
2 (open answer)
3 (open answer)
4 because Toad had no winter clothes and it was cold.
5 (open answer)
6 (open answer)

Thinking it through
(open answer)

UNIT 19 Ready for Winter

Thinking back

Name _____ Date _____

Frog

Toad

Write who said each thing.

1. Come and see how wonderful winter is!

   _____

2. I am in my warm bed.

   _____

3. I do not have any winter clothes.

   _____

4. I have brought you some things to wear.

   _____

5. We will ride down the big hill on my sledge.

   _____

6. Here we go!

   _____

UNIT 19 Ready for Winter

Thinking about it

Name _____ Date _____

Read pupils' book page 21 and answer the questions.

1 Why did Frog call for Toad?
_____

2 Did Frog like winter? How can you tell?
_____
_____

3 Did Toad like winter? How can you tell?
_____
_____

4 Why did Frog bring lots of warm clothes?
_____

5 Why didn't Toad want to go on the sledge?
_____

6 Draw what you think happened at the end of the story.

UNIT 19 Ready for Winter

Thinking it through

Name _____ Date _____

Practise reading this poem about the winter then read the poem to a friend.

Winter Days

Biting air
Winds blow
City streets
Under snow

Noses red
Lips sore
Runny eyes
Hands raw

Chimneys smoke
Cars crawl
Piled snow
On garden wall

Slush in gutters
Ice in lanes
Frosty patterns
On window panes

Morning call
Lift up your head
Nipped by winter
Stay in bed.

1 How are the story on pupils' book page 21 and this poem alike?

   The story and the poem are both about _____ .

2 Which did you like best – the story or the poem? Say why.

   I liked the _____ best because _____

   _____

Focus on Comprehension Teacher's Book 'A'. Poem © Gareth Owen. Text © Louis Fidge 1999
Illustrations © Nelson 1999. Published by Thomas Nelson and Sons Ltd 1999

UNIT 20 Messing About

Starter Book

FURTHER TEACHING OPPORTUNITIES

Text level

Reading comprehension
- Ask children if they ever get into trouble over the state of their bedrooms. Do they ever have any friends in them? What games do they play?
- Look at the title and the illustrations on the page. Ask children to predict what they think the poem is going to be about.
- Read the poem to and with the children several times. During the reading, encourage the use of phonological, contextual, grammatical and graphic knowledge to work out, predict and check the meanings of unfamiliar words and to make sense of what is read. Point out how the patterned and predictable structure of the language helps in reading the text. As the poem becomes more familiar, ask children to join in.
- Ask children for their immediate response to the poem. What did they like (or dislike) about it?
- Look at, and discuss, the way the poem is structured (four verses, with four lines in each verse). Draw attention to the name of the poet.
- Find, read and compare other humorous poems or poems with predictable and patterned language (especially any more poems by Michael Rosen). Encourage children to read them aloud once they become familiar. Collect together a number for a class anthology of favourites.

Writing composition
- Use the poem structure as a model. Play with the idea of alliterative names, such as Bouncing Ben. Encourage the children to substitute a different name in each verse and to think of suitable concluding lines to rhyme.

Sentence level

Grammatical awareness
- The verses could be reproduced with key words omitted. Ask children to suggest a suitable word to go in each gap.
- Encourage the children to read the poem, taking full note of the grammar and punctuation, using pace, tone and expression appropriately.

Sentence construction and punctuation
- Point out how dialogue is shown in the verses. Ask children what each child said.
- Draw attention to the use of question marks in the poem.

Word level

Phonics, word recognition and spelling
- Contrast the words 'mad' and 'made' from the text. Notice what a difference the modifying 'e' (or magic 'e') makes to the sound of the medial vowel. Supply children with a list of other three letter words. Ask them to read them. Add an 'e' to each and ask them to read them again. Discuss the differences. (Some suggested words: cap, tap, fad, pal, Sam, pan, at, pip, win, rid, slim, pin, bit, rob, rod, pop, not, cub, plum, cut.)
- The poem is full of common high frequency words. Provide the children with a list of high frequency words and see which they can find in the poem.

Vocabulary extension
- Use the theme of games. Which games: can be played alone? need more than one person? can be played inside? should be played outside? use a ball? require a bat or racket?
- Write the names of some children in the class. Which have most/least consonants; most/least vowels?

ANSWERS

Thinking back
1. Jumping John had a bellyache.
2. Kicking Kirsty was thirsty.
3. Mad Mickey sat in some glue.
4. Fat Fred hid under the bed.

Thinking about it
Children are asked to re-sequence the lines in the poem to match the poem in the unit.

Thinking it through
(open answers)

UNIT 20 Messing About

Thinking back

Name _____   Date _____

Cut out the pictures.
Match each picture with the correct sentence.

1 I had bellyache.

2 I was thirsty.

3 I sat in some glue.

4 I hid under the bed.

Mad Mickey  | Jumping John | Fat Fred | Kicking Kirsty

UNIT 20 Messing About

Thinking about it

Name _____ Date _____

> The last two lines of each verse have got mixed-up. Write each verse correctly.

"Do you know what?"
said Jumping John.
"I sat in some glue
and I feel all sticky."

"Do you know what?"
said Kicking Kirsty.
"You can't see me,
I'm under the bed."

"Do you know what?"
said Mad Mickey.
"I had a bellyache
and now it's gone."

"Do you know what?"
said Fat Fred.
"All this jumping
has made me thirsty."

UNIT 20 Messing About

Thinking it through

Name _____ Date _____

Can you think of a name beginning with each letter of the alphabet?

Think of a word to go in front of each name that starts with the same letter.

A _____   _____
B _____   _____
C _____   _____
D _____   _____
E _____   _____
F _____Fred_____   _____Fat Fred_____
G _____   _____
H _____   _____
I _____   _____
J _____John_____   _____Jumping John____
K _____Kirsty_____   _____Kicking Kirsty__
L _____   _____
M _____Mickey_____   _____Mad Mickey_____
N _____   _____
O _____   _____
P _____   _____
Q _____   _____
R _____   _____
S _____   _____
T _____   _____
U _____   _____
V _____   _____
W _____   _____
X _____   _____
Y _____   _____
Z _____   _____

Focus on Comprehension Teacher's Book 'A'. Text © Louis Fidge 1999
Illustrations © Nelson 1999. Published by Thomas Nelson and Sons Ltd 1999

Starter Book / Copymaster / Unit 20

UNIT 21 A Visit to the Opticians

Starter Book

FURTHER TEACHING OPPORTUNITIES

Text level

Reading comprehension
- Introduce this unit by asking children to explain ways in which our eyes help us.
- Ask children if this story is true or not. Consider the difference between fiction (which is not imaginary) and non-fiction which is more factual.
- After reading the text, ask children how interesting they found it and what they learnt from it.
- If possible, have a simple reference book on the human body available. Discuss the front and back covers, the book blurb and title, and acquaint children with some of the features of non-fiction books including contents and index pages.

Writing composition
- Ask children to write a few facts they discovered about the work of an optician from the unit.
- Ask children to write an account of a visit to a doctors, dentists or opticians they have made.

Sentence level

Grammatical awareness
- Reproduce some of the sentences from the text, leaving a word out from each for the children to fill in. If the same type of word is omitted each time such as a noun or preposition, this then helps focus on the grammatical functions these words perform.
- Reproduce some simple sentences based on the text but with the words in each sentence in the wrong order. The task is to re-sequence the words so they make proper sentences and make sense.

Sentence construction and punctuation
- Encourage children to make up some questions based on the text. When writing their own questions, ensure the correct use of question marks at the end of each.

Word level

Phonics, word recognition and spelling
- Use the word 'r*oo*m' from the text to focus on the 'oo' phoneme. Brainstorm and list other 'oo' words. The child got some new glasses. Focus on the 'ew' phoneme in the word 'n*ew*'. Brainstorm and list other 'ew' words.
- Use the words 'n*ee*d' and 'r*ea*d' from the text to focus on the medial phonemes. Provide children with ten or so 'ee' and 'ea' words with the medial phonemes missing. Children have to decide which phoneme to use.
- Use the verb 'check' from the text. Notice how it can have 'ing' or 'ed' added. Provide some other regular verbs and suffix them with 'ing' and 'ed'. Look for other 'ing' and 'ed' verbs in books.

Vocabulary extension
- Brainstorm and list the names of other people in the locality who help us in different ways.
- Refer to an information text on the eye and discover the names and functions of some parts of the eye.

ANSWERS

Thinking back

| 1 optician | 2 mum | 3 eyes | 4 letters |
| 5 torch | 6 tests | 7 glasses | 8 see |

Thinking about it
Children are asked to label a picture of the parts of their body with various words (provided on the copymaster).

Thinking it through
An optician looks after our eyes.
A dentist looks after our teeth.
A doctor helps us when we are ill.
A teacher helps us learn.
A hairdresser cuts our hair.
A shop assistant serves us in a shop.
A fire-fighter puts out fires.
A police officer makes sure our town is safe.

UNIT 21 A Visit to the Opticians

Thinking back

Name _____ Date _____

**Look for the answers on page 23 of your book.
Think of a good word to finish each of my sentences.**

1 I went to see the _____ .

2 My _____ went with me.

3 I needed to have my _____ checked.

4 The optician asked me to read some _____ on a chart.

5 The optician shone a _____ in my eyes.

6 The optician did some more _____ .

7 The optician said that I needed to wear _____ .

8 I can _____ a lot better with my new glasses.

UNIT 21 A Visit to the Opticians

Thinking about it

Name _____ Date _____

Label the parts of your body with these words.

head	neck	shoulder	arm	elbow
hand	finger	chest	leg	knee
heel	ankle	foot	toes	eyes

Starter Book / Copymaster / Unit 21

UNIT 21 **A Visit to the Opticians** *Thinking it through*

Name _____   Date _____

Join up the beginning and ending of each sentence.

An optician	helps us learn.
A dentist	serves us in a shop.
A doctor	makes sure our town is safe.
A teacher	looks after our eyes.
A hairdresser	puts out fires.
A shop assistant	looks after our teeth.
A fire-fighter	cuts our hair.
A police officer	helps us when we are ill.

(An optician — looks after our eyes.)

Complete these sentences.

An optician _____.

A dentist _____.

A doctor _____.

A teacher _____.

A hairdresser _____.

A shop assistant _____.

A fire-fighter _____.

A police officer _____.

UNIT 22 Things are Puzzling

Starter Book

FURTHER TEACHING OPPORTUNITIES

Text level

Reading comprehension
- Introduce the unit by getting children to think about the relative sizes of things. Ask if they have ever been up high and looked down from, say, an aeroplane, the top of a tall building. How did things look below? Have they ever stood and looked up at something very tall, such as at the base of the trunk of a tall tree? How did it look?
- The unit is divided into three sections, each section dealing with a small girl meeting a different animal. In each, the animal sees the girl in a different perspective, which she finds very confusing. Study the picture for each section before reading and discussing the text.
- Discuss the nature of each animal Cristina meets and why it views her as it does. Why does Cristina become increasingly puzzled?
- Ask children to retell the passage in their own words. Encourage them to use words like first, next, then, when.
- Where is the story set? Could it really have happened? Do animals really talk?
- Ask children for their opinion of the story.

Writing composition
- What other animals might Cristina have met on her walk? How would they have described her? Brainstorm and list ideas.
- Encourage children to describe the animals Cristina met. Perhaps they could draw a picture of each animal and label it.
- Ask children to make up a story about an adventure in the jungle with 'talking' animals.

Sentence level

Grammatical awareness
- As the story becomes familiar to the children, encourage them to read it aloud with pace, tone and expression, appropriate to the grammar and punctuation, such as pausing at commas and full stops, taking notice of dialogue.
- Reproduce some of the dialogue in the text but introduce inappropriate adjectives, such as: The elephant said, 'You are a very big girl, Cristina.' In the context of the story these sentences will not be meaningful. Ask children to correct them.

Sentence construction and punctuation
- Ask children to find the three questions in the story. Get them to make up some questions of their own about the story and punctuate them correctly.
- Draw attention to the way dialogue is presented in the text. Draw some pictures based on the story with speech bubbles and help children to write appropriate dialogue in each.

Word level

Phonics, word recognition and spelling
- Use the text for letter searches. For example, find all the words – containing a double consonant; double vowel; beginning (or ending) with a certain letter; containing a particular letter pattern (such as 'all').
- Use the text for word searches, such as high frequency words, longest and shortest words.
- Use the verb 'ask' from the text. Notice how it can have 'ing' added as in 'I am asking' or 'ed' as in 'I asked'. Provide some other regular verbs and suffix them with 'ing' and 'ed'. Look for other 'ing' and 'ed' verbs in books.

Vocabulary extension
- Introduce the idea of describing words, by looking at the way each animal described Cristina. Think of other 'size' adjectives to describe different objects or animals. Extend this to work on opposites (see the 'Thinking it through' copymaster).

ANSWERS

Thinking back
1 the elephant   2 Cristina   3 the mouse
4 the giraffe   5 the giraffe   6 Cristina

Thinking about it
(open answers)

Thinking it through
(open answers)

UNIT 22 Things are Puzzling

Thinking back

Name _____ Date _____

| Cristina | the elephant | the mouse | the giraffe |

Write who said each thing.

1. (What is your name?)

   _____

2. (I am a small girl.)

   _____

3. (You are very big.)

   _____

4. (Hallo.)

   _____

5. (You are very short.)

   _____

6. (I am a big small little girl.)

   _____

UNIT 22 Things are Puzzling *Thinking about it*

Name _____ Date _____

1 Why do you think the elephant said Cristina looked small? _____
_____

2 Why do you think the mouse said Cristina looked big? _____
_____

3 Why do you think the giraffe said Cristina looked short? _____
_____

4 Why do you think things were very puzzling to Cristina? _____
_____

5 Cristina met some other animals.
Write how you think Cristina looked to each of these:

a hedgehog   To the hedgehog Cristina looked _____ .

a snake   To the snake Cristina looked _____ .

a tortoise   To the tortoise Cristina looked _____ .

UNIT 22 Things are Puzzling

Thinking it through

Name _____   Date _____

Think of a good word to go in each gap.

1 A _____ is big but a _____ is small.

2 A _____ is long but a _____ is short.

3 A _____ is hard but a _____ is soft.

4 A _____ is smooth but a _____ is prickly.

5 A _____ is sweet but a _____ is sour.

6 A _____ is light but a _____ is heavy.

7 A _____ is wet but a _____ is dry.

8 A _____ is good but a _____ is bad.

9 A _____ is tame but a _____ is wild.

10 A _____ is cold but a _____ is hot.

UNIT 1 Alfie's Feet

Introductory Book

FURTHER TEACHING OPPORTUNITIES

Text level

Reading comprehension
- Consider the sort of character Alfie was. Ask children to consider how old he was. How did he feel at different points in the story? Why did he want to go out again straight away? How did Alfie realise something was wrong?
- Relate the situation to children's own lives. Discuss how they feel when they have got some new clothes or shoes. Do they want to wear them straight away? Do they want to show them off? Why?

Writing composition
- Talk about visits to shoe shops, types of shoes, footwear for different purposes.
- Ask the children to retell the story in the first person, putting themselves in Alfie's place and telling it from his point of view.
- Ask children to write a story about a magic pair of boots. When they are put on, they transport the wearer to any imaginary place they wish to go.

Sentence level

Grammatical awareness
- Ask the children to retell the story in sequence, using structural words such as 'after', 'then', 'next' to help them structure their account.

Sentence construction and punctuation
- When reading the passage aloud, encourage children to notice the use of full stops, commas and exclamation marks. Encourage them to raise their voices expressively when the noise words in the text are read.
- Point out how capital letters are used for emphasis, for people's names and at the beginning of sentences.

Word level

Spelling
- There are many good examples in the passage of words with the suffixes 's' (boots, ducks), 'ing' (stamping, hurrying, turning), 'ed' (walked, wanted, stamped, frightened, looked). Look for these words in the text. Remove the suffixes and note what the root words are.

Vocabulary extension
- Discuss the sound words in the text, and their alliterative features.
- Make lists of different shops and what may be bought in each.

ANSWERS

Thinking back
1. Alfie had some new <u>boots</u>.
2. Alfie went out with <u>Dad</u>.
3. Alfie went to <u>the park</u>.
4. Alfie walked in <u>the mud</u>.

Thinking about it
1. Alfie's boots were very smart and shiny.
2. Alfie wore a mac because it was very wet outside (and might rain again).
3. The ducks hurried back to their pond because Alfie frightened them.
4. Alfie had put his boots on the wrong feet.

Thinking it through
1. (open answer)
2. a) stamp! stamp! stamp!
   b) splish, splash, SPLOSH!
3. a) Birds sing (or tweet).
   b) Ducks quack.
   c) Dogs bark.
   d) Lions roar.
4. (open answer)

▷ *Copymaster* How Would You Feel?
Children are asked to imagine certain everyday situations and to think how they would feel in each.

How Would You Feel?

Name _____   Date _____

How would you feel if ...

... you were allowed to buy any new clothes you wanted?	... you weren't allowed to have a pair of trainers you *really* wanted?
I would feel _____ because _____	I would feel _____ because _____
... you were allowed to wear your best clothes to a party?	... you fell over and tore your favourite pair of jeans?
I would feel _____ because _____	I would feel _____ because _____

> Turn over the page.
> Write about something that would make you feel jealous.

UNIT 2 Mice

Introductory Book

FURTHER TEACHING OPPORTUNITIES

Text level

Reading comprehension
- This short poem lends itself well to being read and reread, and even learnt by heart. Draw attention to the underlying rhythm and rhyming elements.
- Discuss the appealing aspects of mice as well as some of the things that make them disliked by many.

Writing composition
- This poem could lead on to building up a class description of a mouse, or some other pets. Children could write descriptions of their own pets.
- Simple list poems could be written about pets and their characteristics.

Sentence level

Sentence construction and punctuation
- This poem is good for stressing the importance of commas when reading. Notice how some lines have them, and a pause is required, whereas other lines don't end in commas, and one should read on without a pause to make sense.

Word level

Spelling
- There are many phonemes in this poem that could be used as a basis for spelling work such as 'i – e' (mice, white, like); 'igh' (night); 'ee' (teeth), 'ea' (ears); 'ou' (about, house); 'ai' (tails)

Vocabulary extension
- Synonyms for eating could be explored, starting with the word 'nibble'.

ANSWERS

Thinking back
1 True.
2 False.
3 False.
4 True.

Thinking about it
1 Mice have: long tails, small faces, no chins, pink ears, white teeth; they come out at night; they nibble things.

Thinking it through
1 a) mice – nice
   b) small – all
   c) white – night
   d) touch – much
2 (open answer)
3 (open answer which could include owls, badgers, foxes, hedgehogs, moles)
4 'Nocturnal' means that the animal comes out at night.

⇨ *Copymaster* **Monty's Mice**

Monty's Mice is a humorous poem with a predictable language pattern (based on counting) about a rather bizarre mixture of pets that Monty kept in his bedroom. Children are asked to guess what the final mystery pet might be and then to make up a similar poem of their own. They are given the poem's structure to work within.

⇨ Monty's Mice

Name _____ Date _____

In his bedroom, Monty kept
TEN mice with long twitchy whiskers,
NINE big spiders with hairy legs,
EIGHT caterpillars with fat bodies,
SEVEN hamsters that slept all day,
SIX budgies that tweeted in their cage,
FIVE sleek cats that chased the mice,
FOUR scruffy dogs (not very nice!),
THREE snakes who hid under the bed,
TWO gorillas who lived in the wardrobe,
and ONE … GUESS WHAT?

Draw Monty's mystery pet.

Make up a funny poem about some pets you might keep in your bedroom.

In my bedroom, I keep

TEN _____

NINE _____

EIGHT _____

SEVEN _____

SIX _____

FIVE _____

FOUR _____

THREE _____

TWO _____

and ONE _____

Focus on Comprehension Teacher's Book 'A'. Text © Louis Fidge 1999
Illustrations © Nelson 1999. Published by Thomas Nelson and Sons Ltd 1999

Introductory Book / Copymaster / Unit 2

UNIT 3 The Car Ride

Introductory Book

FURTHER TEACHING OPPORTUNITIES

Text level

Reading comprehension
- Discuss the purpose of maps and plans. The picture is somewhere between an aerial view and a simple plan.
- Ask children to relate their experiences of car journeys in the countryside. Discuss some of the things seen in the picture and other things that might be encountered on such a journey.

Writing composition
- The plan is useful for work on giving clear, simple instructions and the use of left and right.
- Imaginative writing could be stimulated by discussing possible adventures based on the map, for example, When Dad fell in the pond!

Sentence level

Grammatical awareness
- Do some work on sequencing, for example, First we passed … and then we saw …

Word level

Spelling
- Compound words could be discussed, using the examples of Bluebell Wood and Riverside Restaurant as starting points.

Vocabulary extension
- Make lists of words such as 'things you would see in the country/town/village'.

ANSWERS

Thinking back
1. The village you pass through is Offley village.
2. The name of the wood is Bluebell Wood.
3. The windmill is on the farm.
4. The pond is near the village.

Thinking about it
Write these sentences in the correct order.
- First we drove through Offley village and saw the church.
- Outside the village we passed a pond.
- Near the pond we saw Bluebell Wood.
- After we turned the first corner there was a farm.
- Soon we went across a bridge over a river.

Thinking it through
1. (open answer)
2. (open answer)
3. (open answer)

➡ Copymaster   The Map
The children are given a simple map and asked to locate and describe the position of various features on it.

The Map

Name _____   Date _____

Look at the map and complete the sentences.

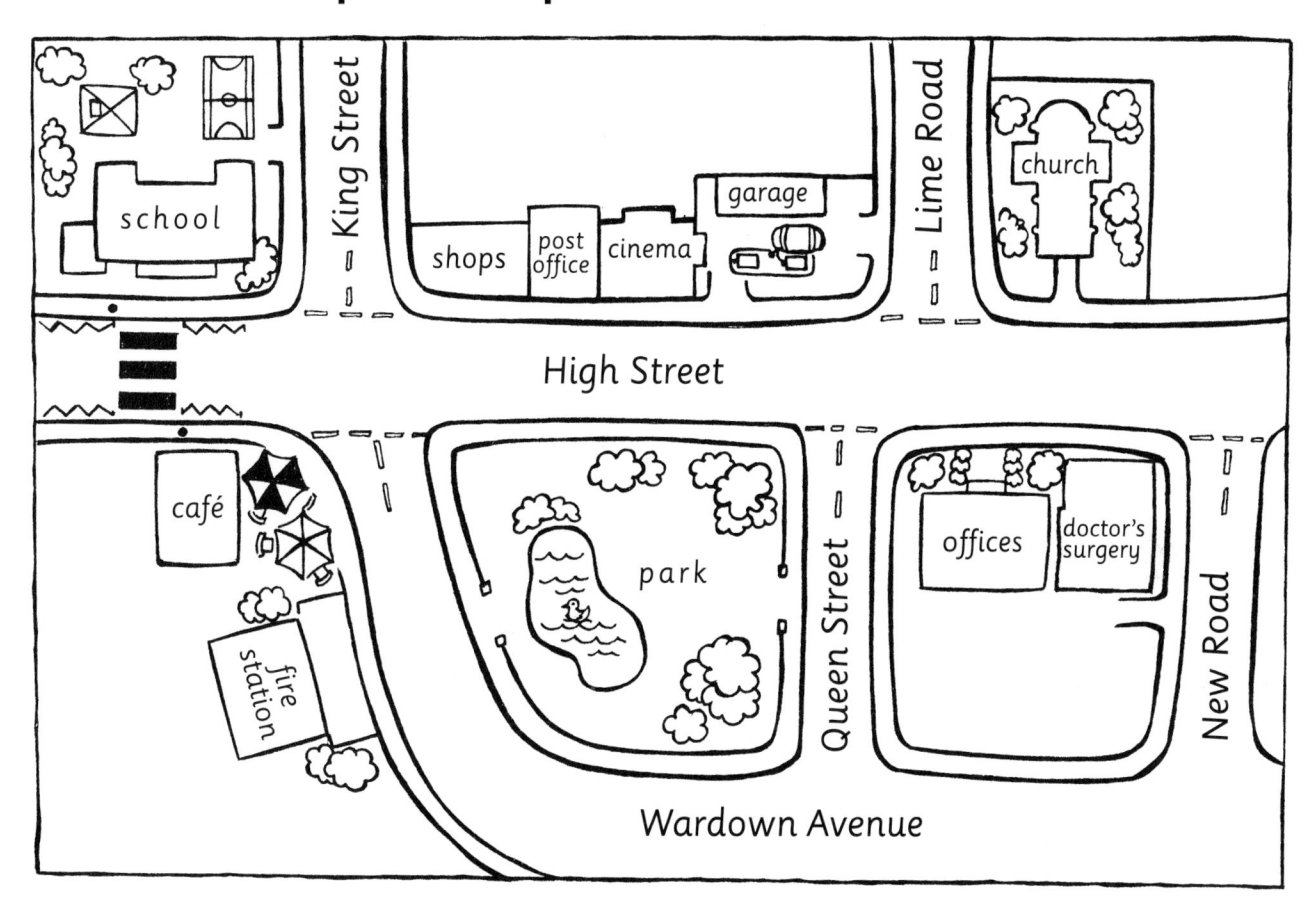

1 The Post Office is between the _____ and the _____ .

2 The garage is on the corner of _____ Road .

3 The school is in _____ Street.

4 Opposite the cinema you will see the _____ .

5 The doctor's surgery is _____ to the offices.

6 The fire station is on _____ Avenue.

7 The café is on the corner of the _____ Street and _____ Avenue.

8 The church is on the corner of the _____ Street and _____ Road.

UNIT 4 Nursery Rhymes Old and New
Introductory Book

FURTHER TEACHING OPPORTUNITIES

Text level

Reading comprehension
- Cause and effect relationships could be explored, using the rhymes, by asking questions such as: 'What happened when … Jack Horner put in his thumb?'
- Contrast the fact that Little Jack Horner is a 'good' boy, whereas Little Sue Horner is cast as a 'naughty' girl. Why is this?
- Collect and read other traditional nursery rhymes (and modern versions, if possible). Also find poems about naughty and good children.

Writing composition
- Have fun making up modern versions of nursery rhymes with the class, or adapting the originals.

Sentence level

Grammatical awareness
- Point out how rhymes help you predict other words such as Horner, corner.

Sentence construction and punctuation
- Capitalisation of people's names can be pointed out, as can the use of capitals at the beginning of new lines, rather than just the beginning of new sentences.

Word level

Spelling
- Phonemes such as 'ea' (eating, sneaks); 'ie' (pie) and 'y' (sly); 'oo' (good) could be investigated.
- Common spelling patterns, such as 'or' and 'er' at the ends of words could be introduced.
- Words that sound the same but are not spelt the same could be discussed such as thumb – plum; pie – sly.

ANSWERS

Thinking back
1. Little Jack Horner <u>sat in the corner</u>.
2. Little Sue Horner was eating <u>crisps</u>.
3. Little Jack Horner put in his thumb and pulled out <u>a plum</u>.
4. Little Sue Horner's mum baked <u>a liver pie</u>.

Thinking about it
1. Little Jack Horner is a boy. Little Sue Horner is a girl.
2. Jack thought he was good because he pulled a plum out of his Christmas pie.
3. (open answer) She probably sneaked round the corner so she would not be seen when she ate her crisps.
4. (open answer) She is being naughty. She should not be eating so near to lunchtime as it will spoil her meal.
5. (open answer)

Thinking it through
1. (Children may have heard Little Jack Horner before and might therefore know of it. Reference to a nursery rhyme book would help prove that it is a traditional rhyme.)
2. (open answer)
3. (open answer)

➡ *Copymaster*
The Wheels on the Car
This poem is based on the old favourite: 'The wheels on the bus go round and round.' The first verse is given to the children. They are then asked to think of suitable noises to complete the other verses.

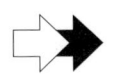

⇨ The Wheels on the Car

Name _____   Date _____

Read (or sing) the first verse of the poem. Think of some noises made by the other parts of the car. Finish off the other verses in your own words.

The wheels on the car go whizz, zoom, screech,
Whizz, zoom, screech, whizz, zoom, screech.
The wheels on the car go whizz, zoom, screech,
All day long.

The engine of the car goes _____
_____
The engine of the car goes _____
All day long.

The doors on the car go _____
_____
_____
All day long.

The horn on the car goes _____
_____
_____
All day long.

UNIT 5 Making a Peanut Butter and Jam Sandwich

Introductory Book

FURTHER TEACHING OPPORTUNITIES

Text level

Reading comprehension
- This unit is good for discussing characteristics of instructional language, for instance, a clear statement of purpose at the start, sequential steps set out as a list, direct language.
- Discuss how helpful the page layout is (for instance numbered steps with a picture illustrating each step).
- Look for, and read, other sets of instructions – in the classroom, in technology books, recipes, and so on.

Writing composition
- Use the unit as a scaffold to help children compose and write their own sets of instructions, such as for getting to school, playing noughts and crosses.
- Encourage children to use illustrations and diagrams to support their own written instructions, and to use direct, concise language.

Sentence level

Grammatical awareness
- When discussing instructions and directions, encourage the use of structural language to help sequencing, such as 'firstly', 'next', 'during'.

Sentence construction and punctuation
- Experiment with different ways of writing instructions. For making the sandwich, try setting out the instructions as a flow diagram, using boxes and arrows.

Word level

Spelling
- The two different sound values of the vowel phoneme 'ea' could be considered (as in 'read' and 'bread').
- Compound words, such as 'peanut', 'into' and 'another' could be identified.

Vocabulary extension
- Butter comes in packets or tubs. How else is food packaged (such as tinned or boxed)? Why? Think about the linkage between the type of food and its packaging.

ANSWERS

Thinking back
Copy and complete these sentences.
When you make a peanut <u>butter</u> and <u>jam</u> sandwich you need two slices of <u>bread</u>. You need a <u>knife</u> to cut the bread into sandwiches. You also need a jar of <u>peanut</u> butter and a <u>jar</u> of jam to spread on the bread.

Thinking about it
1. You need some bread, a knife, some peanut butter and some jam.
2. The first thing you do is spread the peanut butter on one slice of bread.
3. After this you spread some jam on the peanut butter.
4. The third thing you do is place another slice of bread on top.
5. The last thing you do is cut the bread, and then eat the sandwich.

Thinking it through
1. (open answer)
2. (open answer)
3. (open answer)

➡ *Copymaster*   The Rope Swing
The children are given a series of six pictures and are asked to cut them out and sequence them in the correct order to tell the story. They are then asked to write a sentence about each picture.

:➡️ **The Rope Swing**

Name _____   Date _____

Cut out the pictures. Put them in the correct order to tell the story. Write a sentence about each picture.

UNIT 6 Granny, Granny, Please Comb my Hair

Introductory Book

FURTHER TEACHING OPPORTUNITIES

Text level

Reading comprehension
- Identify and describe the three characters in the poem. What can be learnt about them, and inferred from the text or illustrations?
- Find and read other poems about family and friends.
- Draw attention to terms such as poem, poet, verse, rhyme in relation to the poems that the children have read.

Writing composition
- What 'special' people do the children have in their lives? What sorts of things do they do with them? Encourage children to write anecdotally about their experiences. Brainstorm and collect key words, writing them on the board. Allow children to use these as a basis for writing a description or list poem (it doesn't have to rhyme!) about someone special.

Sentence level

Grammatical awareness
- Note how the poem is addressed to Granny personally and is written and expressed in the second person 'you' most of the time.

Sentence construction and punctuation
- Interestingly, there is little punctuation in the poem. The normal conventions of commas are not obeyed where they occur at the ends of lines where a pause is required, nor full stops at the ends of sentences.

Word level

Spelling
- Focus on phonemes 'ee' (knees, breeze); 'ea' (head); 'air' (hair); 'are' (care); 'ar' (parting); 'ur' (turn); 'ir' (girl).

Vocabulary extension
- Contrast the fact that Granny always takes her time, whereas Mummy is always in a rush. This could lead on to discussing opposites (antonyms). Use some of the words in the poem as a starting point, for instance, gentle – rough; girl – boy; finish – begin; always – never.

ANSWERS

Thinking back
1 The girl wants Granny to <u>comb her hair</u>.
2 Granny sits the girl <u>on a cushion</u>.
3 Granny always takes a lot of <u>care</u>.
4 The girl's mum is always <u>in a rush</u>.

Thinking about it
1 The girl likes it because Granny takes her time, always takes care and tells the girl she's a nice girl.
2 The girl doesn't like her mum combing her hair because she is always in a rush and she sometimes tugs.
3 (open answer)

Thinking it through
1 (open answer) Some reasons could be that Granny always takes her time and tells the girl she's nice.
2 (open answer)
3 (open answer)

➡ *Copymaster* **My Grannies**
Two grannies are contrasted in this poem – one the poet likes and one she dislikes. The children are asked to complete some sentences about the poem and then to consider which grandmother is most like the gran in the poem in Unit 6.

➡️ My Grannies

Name _____ Date _____

My Grannies

I hate it, in the holiday,
When Grandma brings her pets to stay –
Her goat, her pig, her seven rats
Scare our dog and chase our cats.
Her budgies bite, her parrots shout –
And guess who has to clean them out?

My other Gran, the one I like,
Always brings her motor bike,
And when she takes me for a ride
To picnic in the countryside,
We zoom up hills and whizz round bends –
I hate it when her visit ends!

1 Grandma comes during the _____

2 Here are the pets she brings: _____

3 Her parrots _____

4 The poet does not like the pets because _____

5 My other Gran brings her _____

6 We go for a _____ in the countryside.

7 We _____ up hills and _____ round bends.

8 Which grandmother is most like the one in Unit 6?
   Write and say why. _____
   _____
   _____

Focus on Comprehension Teacher's Book 'A'. Poem © June Crebbin 1988
Text © Louis Fidge 1999. Illustrations © Nelsons 1999
Published by Thomas Nelson and Sons Ltd 1999

Introductory Book / Copymaster / Unit 6

UNIT 7 Willy and Hugh

Introductory Book

FURTHER TEACHING OPPORTUNITIES

Text level

Reading comprehension
- Allow the children to act out the story as a means to retelling it.
- Discuss the themes of loneliness, making friends, feeling excluded, fear, and so on, in relation to the story and their own experiences.

Writing composition
- Write character profiles of Willy and Hugh from information provided and gained by inference.
- Hugh, big as he was, feared spiders. Discuss and write about frightening experiences and common fears.
- The theme of bullies getting their comeuppance (as Buster Nose does in the story) could be used as a basis for composing similar simple stories.

Sentence level

Grammatical awareness
- The story contains a good variety of punctuation marks. Read the story taking these into account, and raise awareness of how the meaning affects reading with expression.

Sentence construction and punctuation
- Note the use of speech marks and how they are used.
- Notice, too, how the author uses capital letters to emphasise words on one occasion: TERRIFYING CREATURE.

Word level

Spelling
- Use words from the passage to draw attention to how we add suffixes to some words to change their meaning. There are many:
  - simple plurals made when 's' is added – friends, games, joggers
  - verbs to which 'ing' or 'ed' have been added – seemed, walking, minding, enjoying, appeared, looking, laughed, asked.
- Introduce the concept of syllables to children, by tapping out the syllables of words as you say them. There are many multi-syllabic words in the text.

Vocabulary extension
- Ask the children to find five words they particularly like from the story and to explain why they like them.

ANSWERS

Thinking back
Willy had no <u>friends</u>. No-one let him join in any of their <u>games</u>. One day Willy met Hugh Jape in the <u>park</u>. They sat down on a <u>bench</u> and watched the joggers. When they were in the <u>library</u> Hugh Jape was <u>frightened</u> by a spider. Willy <u>moved</u> the spider. <u>Willy</u> and Hugh Jape became good friends.

Thinking about it
1 No-one let Willy join in their games. They all said he was useless.
2 They met each other in the park. (Hugh Jape bumped into Willy.)
3 You can tell Buster Nose was a bully by the way he talked to Willy and by what he said.
4 Hugh scared Buster away.
5 Willy rescued Hugh from a spider.

Thinking it through
1 Willy probably felt very lonely, because he had no friends and no one would play with him.
2 Willy probably felt a lot happier because he had made a new friend – Hugh.
3 (open answer)

➥ *Copymaster* The Bullies
Children are given six sentences to sequence to tell the beginning of a story with a bullying theme. They are then asked to write a few sentences to continue the story.

The Bullies

Name _____   Date _____

Put these sentences in the correct order. Then write a few sentences and continue the story in your book.

| I heard them come up behind me, sniggering and giggling. |

| I noticed the two children standing by the railings as I passed. |

| I tried not to let them see I was scared and wondered what to do next. |

| They tried to bump into me and began to call me names. |

| I was late coming out of school, so all my friends had gone. |

| I thought I had better not shout back so I hurried on. |

UNIT 8 The Hare and the Tortoise

Introductory Book

FURTHER TEACHING OPPORTUNITIES

Text level

Reading comprehension
- Use the story to develop an understanding of the importance of sequence. Ask 'What happened when …?' questions.
- Explore the differences in character between the Hare and the Tortoise.
- What moral can be learned from the story? Read and compare other fables and consider their morals.

Writing composition
- Ask children to make up their own stories along the same lines. Use picture frames to help support their writing.

Sentence level

Grammatical awareness
- Practise changing verbs into the past tense. Use a simple sentence structure to help, such as:
I run a race. Yesterday I ran a race.
I sleep in my bed. Yesterday I slept in my bed.
I catch a ball. Yesterday I caught a ball.

Sentence construction and punctuation
- Notice the way this story is presented as a series of pictures and sentence captions. Look at other picture books and comics. Note other conventions commonly associated with picture books such as the use of speech bubbles.

Word level

Spelling
- Do word hunts. Ask the children to look for words containing common letter strings to reinforce spelling points, such as 'are', 'oi', 'or', double consonants.

Vocabulary extension
- The story is good for reinforcing work on antonyms, such as fast/slow; awake/asleep; walk/run; win/lose.

ANSWERS

Thinking back
1. Hare boasted because he could run fast.
2. Tortoise could only walk slowly.
3. Hare decided to have a sleep.
4. Tortoise passed Hare and won the race.

Thinking about it
1. Hare asked Tortoise for a race because he was bored and wanted some fun.
2. It was not a fair race because Hare could run much faster than Tortoise.
3. (open answer) Hare was a show-off because he was always boasting.
4. (open answer)

Thinking it through
1. The moral is: 'Don't give up. Always keep trying.'
2. a) hot – cold
   b) asleep – awake
   c) hard – soft or easy
   d) heavy – light
   e) win – lose
3. Perseverance means 'keep on trying and don't give up'. In the story, Tortoise had perseverance.

▶ *Copymaster*   The Jar of Sweets
This is a cloze procedure activity based on a modern version of an Aesop's fable with a clear moral about the problems of being greedy.

The Jar of Sweets

Name _____ Date _____

Think of a sensible word to fill in each gap.

A greedy boy saw a jar of _____ standing on a table.

He licked _____ lips and reached _____ the jar.

He put his _____ in and grabbed the biggest handful he could _____. The problem was _____ the boy had picked _____ so many sweets that he could not _____ his hand _____ of the jar.

He _____ angrily. If he let the _____ go he would be _____ to take his hand out of the jar. But he wanted those sweets so _____!

A friend saw him and gave him _____ advice. 'Don't be so _____,' the friend said. 'If you only take _____ sweet at a time your hand will come out of the jar _____.'

UNIT 9 About Books

Introductory Book

FURTHER TEACHING OPPORTUNITIES

Text level

Reading comprehension
- Discuss the differences between fact and fiction and non-fiction books.
- Consider what information the covers of books can give us. Look at several different books from the library. How do the pictures, titles, book blurbs help us? What sorts of books are they? What might they be about? Scan the contents pages and indexes to confirm opinions.

Sentence level

Sentence construction and punctuation
- Note how capital letters are used in titles of books and in people's names.

Word level

Spelling
- Use the titles of books for reinforcing work on syllables. Read any multi-syllabic words slowly and listen to them carefully. Tap out the syllables in them and count them, for instance, in – sect (2 syllables); ad – ven – ture (3 syllables). Consider how this could help to spell the words.

Vocabulary extension
- Discuss what people are involved in producing books such as author, poet, illustrator, publisher.
- Think of words associated with books – covers, titles, contents, chapters.
- Categorise different types of fiction (poetry, story books) and non-fiction books (information, encyclopaedias, telephone directories). Sort piles of books into types.

ANSWERS

Thinking back
1. The title of the story book is *The Big Adventure*.
2. The title of the information book is *All about insects*.
3. Ruby Clarke wrote *All about insects*.
4. Roger Stevens illustrated *The Big Adventure*.

Thinking about it
1. An author is someone who writes books.
2. An illustrator is someone who draws the pictures in books.
3. (open answer) Illustrators make the book look interesting.
4. Book titles give you an idea what is in the book.
5. A non-fiction book is an information book.
6. A story book is a fiction book.

Thinking it through
1. (open answer)
2. (open answer)
3. (open answer) An encyclopaedia is a book containing lots of facts and information about many different things.
4. (open answer) A dictionary is used for finding the meanings of words and for checking their spellings. It is a non-fiction book.

➡ *Copymaster* **Using a Dictionary**
Children are given a list of 's' words, arranged in alphabetical order with their accompanying definitions. They are asked to find and write the definitions for some of the words given. They are then asked to use a dictionary to find some more 's' words and write definitions of their own for them.

⇨ Using a Dictionary

Name _____   Date _____

- **saddle** a seat for a rider on a horse
- **scarf** a long piece of cloth worn round the neck
- **sentry** a soldier on guard
- **shamrock** a plant with green leaves that are in three parts
- **signal** a message or sign telling you what to do
- **skeleton** all the 206 bones of the body
- **slug** a kind of snail without a shell
- **smile** a happy look on your face
- **snarl** a low, growling noise
- **somersault** to turn over and over, head over heels
- **spike** a large, sharp point
- **square** a shape with four equal sides
- **stork** a bird with a long beak and long legs

Write the definition of

shamrock _____

snarl _____

somersault _____

sentry _____

spike _____

square _____

Now use a dictionary to help you write a definition for

stallion _____

shepherd _____

scarce _____

syrup _____

submarine _____

UNIT 10 Bedtime

Introductory Book

FURTHER TEACHING OPPORTUNITIES

Text level

Reading comprehension
- Read the poem aloud, in a slightly wheedling, whining tone and raise the pitch of your voice at the end of each question. Comment on the importance of understanding punctuation when reading aloud.
- Discuss the poem's setting and relate it to the children's own experiences.
- Find and read other poems involving children and adults.

Writing composition
- Brainstorm and list other excuses children often make or reasons given for wanting to stay up late. As a class, make them into a collective poem.

Sentence level

Sentence construction and punctuation
- Notice the use of question and exclamation marks and commas in the poem. Discuss when and why they are used.
- Some children may notice the apostrophes used for contraction in many words, such as you've, can't. If appropriate, explain what they stand for.

Word level

Spelling
- Find words that rhyme in the poem and note that, whilst they may sound the same, they are not necessarily spelt the same such as four, floor, more.

ANSWERS

Thinking back
1 On the floor, the child was building <u>a castle</u>.
2 The child was reading <u>a book</u>.
3 The child was making <u>a bead chain</u>.
4 The child had just started playing <u>a game</u>.

Thinking about it
1 The child said that if you don't finish a game you never find out who has lost or won.
2 (open answer) The child was probably talking to his or her mother or father.
3 (open answer)

Thinking it through
1 Which words have a similar meaning to 'asking'?
   requesting   begging
2 (open answer)
3 (open answer)

▶ *Copymaster   Bedtime Lullaby*
Children are given a bedtime lullaby, with some words in Gaelic and Welsh. This is followed by some literal questions based on the text and a couple of inferential questions.

Bedtime Lullaby

Name _____ Date _____

Cushlamochree, O Cushlamochree[1],
Shall you dance for the stars?
Shall you play with the sea?
Shall you swim like a whale?
Shall you follow the sun?
O Cushlamochree, has your dreaming begun?

Cariad Bach, O Cariad Bach[2],
Shall you sing to the moon?
Shall you shout for the dark?
Shall you whisper with bears?
Shall you waken the night?
O Cariad Bach, soft dreams and sleep tight.

[1] Cushlamochree is Gaelic for 'darling'.
[2] Cariad Bach is Welsh for 'little darling'.

1 What shall you dance for? _____

2 What shall you follow? _____

3 What shall you sing to? _____

4 What shall you whisper with? _____

5 What does Cushlamochree mean? _____

6 In what language does Cariad Bach mean 'little darling'? _____

7 Explain what a lullaby is. _____

8 Who do you think is asking the questions? _____

UNIT 11　Face to Face with a Dragon

Introductory Book

FURTHER TEACHING OPPORTUNITIES

Text level

Reading comprehension
- There are many words which may be unfamiliar to children in the text, such as 'processions', 'confusion'. Encourage the use of different cues to help them work out possible meanings for them. Dictionaries could be used to confirm their ideas.
- Discuss the context of the story. Ask children to make suggestions to flesh out details about the setting and characters in the story.
- Point out how the writer uses repeated words for emphasis such as 'round and round, down, down, down'.

Writing composition
- Ask the children to extend the story and write their own ending to it.
- Focus on the excitement of celebrations – the noise words, the colour, the activities. Encourage children to write about a celebration they have attended.

Sentence level

Grammatical awareness
- There are several sentences that contain 'joining' words (conjunctions) in the text, for example, Chin Chiang pulled her by the hand, and they hurried down the stairs together. Find these and rewrite them as two separate sentences, noting any changes that occur.

Sentence construction and punctuation
- Draw attention to the use of commas, some signalling a pause and others separating words in lists in the text.

Word level

Spelling
- Focus on compound words, using the word 'firecrackers' as a starting point, for instance, fireworks, fireplace, firefighters, firelight.

- Use the words 'colourful' and 'suddenly'. Encourage children to think of other words with the same suffixes. (Point out that 'ful' only has one 'l' when used as a suffix.)
- The text is packed with opportunities for 'phoneme fun'. Give a phoneme and set children to find words containing it such as 'ou', 'ow'.

Vocabulary extension
- List some common celebrations: birthdays, weddings or religious occasions such as Christmas, Id. Ask children to supply words associated with them.

ANSWERS

Thinking back
1 Chin Chiang and Pu Yee went down the <u>stairs</u> together.
2 Chin Chiang and Pu Yee went down to the <u>market</u> street.
3 They heard the sound of <u>firecrackers</u> exploding.
4 Chin Chiang let go of Pu Yee's <u>hand</u>.
5 Chin Chiang came face to face with a <u>dragon</u>.

Thinking about it
1 Chinese people have colourful processions and festivals to celebrate their New Year. They often dress up as dragons and dance through the streets.
2 Chin Chiang was a boy.
3 Chin Chiang lived upstairs.
4 (open answer)

Thinking it through
1 It means there was a lot of noise and excitement.
2 (open answer)
3 (open answer)

▶ *Copymaster*
The Chinese Calendar
Children are told that years in the Chinese calendar are named after different animals and given a grid listing the animals and their characteristics. The questions that follow require the children to look for information contained in the grid.

The Chinese Calendar

Name _____   Date _____

Each year is named after an animal in the Chinese calendar. Some people believe that you take on the characteristics of the animal in whose year you are born.

Animal	Year	Characteristics
Rabbit	1999	Patient and shy
Dragon	2000	Energetic, talkative and healthy
Snake	2001	Wise, careful, wealthy
Horse	2002	Clever and popular
Ram	2003	Gentle and artistic. Inclined to worry
Monkey	2004	Creative and curious
Cockerel	2005	Proud, good at writing and music
Dog	2006	Honest and helpful
Pig	2007	Polite and dependable
Rat	2008	Cheerful and kind, makes friends easily.
Ox	2009	Calm, quiet and strong
Tiger	2010	Brave and powerful

1 Which year is named after:

a) a snake? _____   b) a dog? _____

c) a horse? _____   d) a rabbit? _____

2 Which animals are these years named after:

a) 2007? _____   b) 2003? _____

c) 2000? _____   d) 1999? _____

3 Which animals have the following characteristics:

a) patient and shy? _____   b) creative and curious? _____

c) honest and helpful? _____   d) clever and popular? _____

4 Which animal comes after:

a) the tiger? _____   b) the cockerel? _____

c) the rat? _____   d) the pig? _____

UNIT 12 Contents and Index Pages

Introductory Book

FURTHER TEACHING OPPORTUNITIES

Text level

Reading comprehension
- Discuss where contents and index pages may be found in books. Discuss their purpose. Note how the pages are arranged and other characteristics of the pages, such as page numbers are given, the use of alphabetical order, the way pages are set out in columns to aid reading.
- Use contents and index pages of books from the library for finding a way about the books, to find particular topics or sections.

Sentence level

Sentence construction and punctuation
- Pose questions requiring children to construct simple sentences, based on using contents and index pages of different books, such as: 'Where will you find … Who is … Why are …?'

Word level

Spelling
- The more common sounds of consonant digraphs may be explored, using words such as 'dishwasher', 'chairs', 'telephone' from the text. Some children might spot the word 'machine'. This could provide an opportunity to discuss more unusual pronunciations of 'ch' as in 'machine', 'Christmas'.
- The words in the contents and index lists shown also provide many possible jumping off points for spelling work based on phonemes and common letter patterns.

Vocabulary extension
- Lists of words linked to particular topics could be drawn up, based on the material in the unit, such as: food, furniture, water.

ANSWERS

Thinking back
1. washing machines (page 22)
2. televisions (page 7)
3. watches and clocks (page 24)
4. telephones (page 4)
5. vacuum cleaners (page 20)

Thinking about it
1. cereals (Food – page 25)
2. chairs (Furniture – page 30)
3. drains (Water, taps and toilets – page 17)
4. electricity (Lights – page 10)
5. aerials (Televisions – page 7)

Thinking it through
1. A contents page tells you how some books are organised.
2. (open answer)
3. You would find an index page at the back of a book.
4. A contents page tells you how a book is organised. An index tells you where to find things.
5. An index is arranged in alphabetical order. This helps you to find things more quickly.
6. (open answer – examples: dictionary, an encyclopaedia, a telephone directory)

➡ *Copymaster* **A Glossary**
This sheet explains what a glossary is, gives an extract from one and asks children to answer questions based on it.

➡ A Glossary

Name _____ Date _____

> Some books contain a glossary at the end. This is a list of any special words used in the book and their meanings. Here is part of a glossary from an English book:

comma	A **comma** is a punctuation mark. It tells you to pause.
exclamation	An **exclamation** is a sentence which shows that we feel something strongly. It always ends with an **exclamation mark**.
full stop	A **full stop** is a dot showing that a sentence has ended.
question	A **question** is what we ask when we want to know something. Questions always end with a question mark.
sentence	A **sentence** should make sense on its own. It should begin with a capital letter. Most sentences end with a full stop.

1 What is a glossary? _____

_____

2 In which part of a book would you find a glossary? _____

_____

3 Are the words in the glossary organised in alphabetical order?

_____

4 Explain what a sentence is. _____

_____

5 Explain when you would use a question mark. _____

_____

6 If you see a comma when you are reading, what should you do?

_____

UNIT 13 The Blind Men and the Elephant

Introductory Book

FURTHER TEACHING OPPORTUNITIES

Text level

Reading comprehension
- This story is good for sequencing activities. Focus on the use of structure words indicating the order of events.

Writing composition
- There are many other stories of a similar genre that contain a lot of repetition such as the Gingerbread Man, The Great Big Turnip, Henny Penny. Read and tell some of these and discuss their structure. Encourage children to write their own stories, based on repetitive and predictable events.
- Shadows at night often appear to take on other characteristics. Allow the children to talk about their own experiences.
- Compose some simple sentences about blindness, for example: What would you miss most if you were blind?

Sentence level

Grammatical awareness
- When reading the text, point out the use of speech marks, demarcating what each blind man said.

Sentence construction and punctuation
- Turn some of the statements in the text into questions, using 'wh' words. For example, Who is the story about? What did the ... Where are ... Why did ...

Word level

Spelling
- Notice the difference in the pronunciation of the 'ea' in 'ear' and 'head'. Think of other examples.
- Use the word 'elephant' to discuss 'ph' words.

Vocabulary extension
- Use the structure 'a _____ is like a _____' and apply it to parts of other animals.

ANSWERS

Thinking back
1. The first blind man touched its trunk.
2. The second blind man touched its tusks.
3. The third blind man touched its ear.
4. The fourth blind man touched its leg.
5. The fifth blind man touched its side.
6. The sixth blind man touched its tail.

Thinking about it
1. It says the men were blind.
2. Each man said the elephant was something different because he touched a different part of the animal.
3. They all argued with each other because each one thought he was right.
4. 'In a way, they were all partly right' means that what each one said was a good guess, given that each had only been able to feel a part of the elephant.

Thinking it through
1. (open answer)
2. (open answer) We can learn not to jump to conclusions. We can learn to listen to other people's views and try to make sense of them all.
3. (open answer)

▶ *Copymaster* **Riddles**
Children are given six riddles with three clues each and are asked to draw and write the correct answer to each.

Riddles

Name _____   Date _____

Draw and write the answer to these riddles:

1 I have a long tail. I have a pouch. I jump. I am a _____ .	**2** I have two hands. I have a face. I help you tell the time. I am a _____ .
3 You lick me. You write on me. You put a stamp on me. I am an _____ .	**4** I come out at night. You can see me in the sky. I hoot. I am an _____ .
5 You put clothes in me. You lock me. You take me on holiday. I am a _____ .	**6** I have wings. I can fly. I am made of metal. I am an _____ .

UNIT 14 From a Tadpole to a Frog

Introductory Book

FURTHER TEACHING OPPORTUNITIES

Text level

Reading comprehension
- Discuss how the life of the frog is cyclical in nature. Note how the pictures of the different stages are linked by arrows to emphasise this.
- Ask children to describe the differences in each picture as the tadpole becomes a frog.

Writing composition
- Find out more about frogs and ask children to write some non-chronological reports about them. For example, They live in …, They eat …
- Use reference books to discover more about other animals' life cycles, such as butterflies and moths. Based on the example in the book, get children to represent these as a set of pictures and sentences, linked by arrows.

Sentence level

Grammatical awareness
- Use the text as a chance to introduce the idea of grammatical agreement. Compare and note differences in 'A frog lays its eggs in water' and 'Frogs lay their eggs in water'. Use simple sentences to reinforce the point, linked to animal movements. 'A horse gallops' but 'horses gallop'.
- The verbs in the text are all written in the present tense. Read the text again as if it happened yesterday and discuss what happens to the verbs.

Sentence construction and punctuation
- Ask children to make up their own questions, based on statements from the text such as: 'Where does a frog lay its eggs?'

Word level

Spelling
- Consider the links between the 'aw' and 'or' phonemes in words such as crawl and short.

Vocabulary extension
- Use a dictionary to check and write meanings for unusual words in the text such as spawn, hatch.

ANSWERS

Thinking back
1. A frog lays its eggs in <u>water</u>.
2. Frogs' eggs are called <u>spawn</u>.
3. Out of the eggs come <u>tadpoles</u>.
4. Each tadpole grows two back <u>legs</u>.
5. The tadpole's tail gets <u>shorter</u>.
6. Tadpoles turn into <u>frogs</u>.

Thinking about it
First the frog lays its eggs.
Next the tadpoles come out of the eggs.
Then each tadpole grows two back legs.
After this it grows two front legs.
When it becomes a frog it comes out of the water.

Thinking it through
1. 'Hatch' means when the tadpole comes out of the egg.
2. (open answer) Both start life looking nothing like the thing they grow into – a tadpole grows into a frog and a caterpillar grows into a butterfly.
3. (open answer)

▷ *Copymaster* Labelling
Children are given a brief text about insects and are asked to label a picture based on information given and by using deduction.

⇨ Labelling

Name _____   Date _____

Insects come in lots of different shapes and sizes, but they all have some things that are the same. They all have six legs. An insect's body has three parts: the head, the thorax (the middle) and the abdomen.

Write these labels in the correct boxes below.

| eye | head | leg | thorax | antenna | abdomen |

Focus on Comprehension Teacher's Book 'A'. Text © Louis Fidge 1999
Illustrations © Nelson 1999. Published by Thomas Nelson and Sons Ltd 1999

Introductory Book / Copymaster / Unit 14

UNIT 15 A Dark, Dark Tale

Introductory Book

FURTHER TEACHING OPPORTUNITIES

Text level

Reading comprehension
- Discuss the form and layout of the poem. Note how the repetition of the word 'dark' heightens the rather menacing feeling. The poem is rather like a long camera shot which gradually focuses in.
- Discuss the ending. Was it a surprise? Consider and substitute other possible endings.
- Ask what other repetitive stories or poems the children know, such as The House that Jack Built.

Writing composition
- Write other similar poems, using the same format. Experiment with changing the adjective, the setting or the ending.
- Get children to write some anecdotal experiences or thoughts about darkness or night-time.
- Produce a class list poem on 'Darkness is…'.

Sentence level

Grammatical awareness
- The poem is ideal for reading aloud with expression. It could lend itself to choral work, with different groups taking different verses and all joining in the last verse.
- There are many prepositions used. Draw attention to them ('on, in, at the front, behind, up, across' and so on).

Sentence construction and punctuation
- Note the use of the commas and the use of capitalisation for emphasis.
- Ask children to turn some of the statements into questions, using a range of 'wh' words such as, 'Where was the dark, dark wood?' 'What was in the dark, dark wood?'

Word level

Spelling
- The poem is full of potential for work on different phonemes, such as 'ar', 'oo', 'ou', 'ai', 'oa', 'or', 'er'.

Vocabulary extension
- Try to think of as many 'dark' words as possible.

ANSWERS

Thinking back
1 On the dark, dark moor there was a <u>dark, dark wood</u>.
2 In the dark, dark wood there was a <u>dark, dark house</u>.
3 In the dark, dark hall there were some <u>dark, dark stairs</u>.
4 In the corner there was a dark, dark <u>box</u>.
5 In the box there was a <u>mouse</u>.

Thinking about it
1 The mouse was in a dark, dark box. The box was in a dark, dark corner. The corner was in a dark, dark cupboard. The dark, dark cupboard was in a dark, dark room. There was a dark, dark curtain in front of the doorway to the dark, dark room. The dark, dark curtain was along a dark, dark passage. The dark, dark passage was at the top of some dark, dark stairs. The dark, dark stairs were in a dark, dark hall. The dark, dark hall was behind a dark, dark door. The dark, dark door was at the front of a dark, dark house. The dark, dark house was in a dark, dark wood. The dark, dark wood was on a dark, dark moor.

Thinking it through
1 (open answer)
2 (open answer)
3 (open answer)

▷ *Copymaster* Who's There?
Children are given the first verse of a poem characterised by patterned language and a predictable pattern. They are asked to complete the missing part of each verse, using context clues and deduction.

Who's There?

Name _____ Date _____

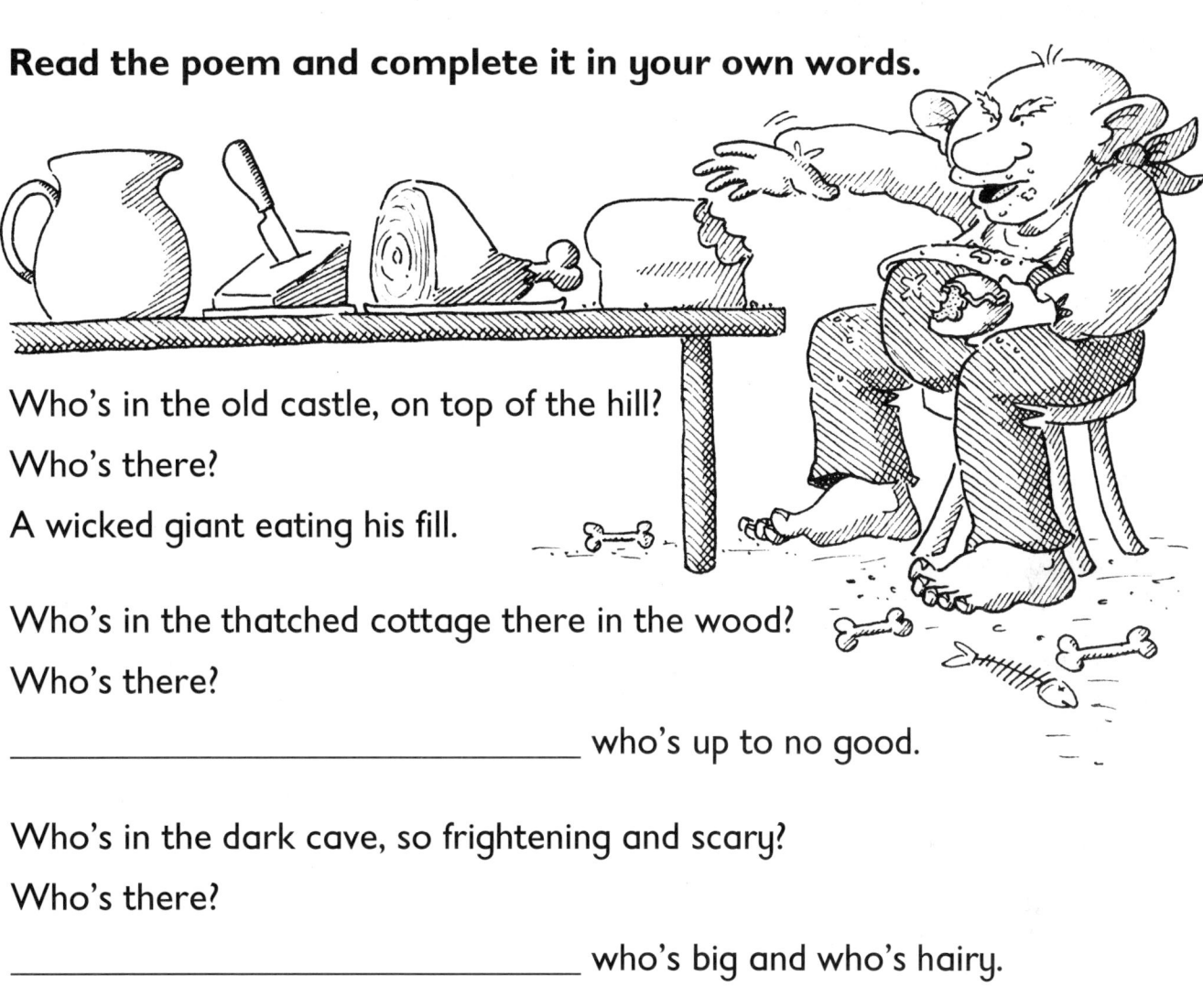

Read the poem and complete it in your own words.

Who's in the old castle, on top of the hill?
Who's there?
A wicked giant eating his fill.

Who's in the thatched cottage there in the wood?
Who's there?
_____ who's up to no good.

Who's in the dark cave, so frightening and scary?
Who's there?
_____ who's big and who's hairy.

Who's sitting and croaking on that old log?
Who's there?
He's fat and green. _____

Who's hiding down there in the ditch?
Who's there?
She's casting spells _____ .

Who's galloping along with a cloak, gold and red?
Who's there?
It's _____ with a crown on his head.

UNIT 16 Mr Cosmo the Conjuror

Introductory Book

FURTHER TEACHING OPPORTUNITIES

Text level

Reading comprehension
- Read other books by Allan Ahlberg and compare them. See what can be found out about this author.
- Consider how the author builds up a feeling of suspense and mystery. (Note the use of short sentences.)
- There are several strange happenings in the story. Ask children to use their imagination to try and offer explanations.

Writing composition
- Make posters for Mr Cosmo.
- Ask children to write about a time when they visited a circus or saw a magician.
- Write a description of how Mr Cosmo might have looked and draw a picture.

Sentence level

Grammatical awareness
- Ask children to retell the events in the passage in sequence, using appropriate structural words, such as 'first, next, then, after this'.
- Experiment by changing the number of animals mentioned and seeing what happens to the accompanying verbs, such as 'A dog was chasing it': 'Some dogs were chasing it.'

Sentence construction and punctuation
- Point out and discuss the use of capitalisation and italics for effect. Note, too, the use of exclamation marks denoting surprise, and the use of commas to separate items in a list.

Word level

Spelling
- There are several verbs ending in 'ed' and 'ing' that could be investigated, to see what happens to the root word when the suffix is added.
- See what compound words can be found in the text.

- Do some work on syllabification, tapping out each syllable as the words are spoken slowly.
- Try adding some adverbs to sentences, such as, 'The door opened slowly.' Consider the spelling of adverbs ending in 'ly'.

Vocabulary extension
- List people who work in circuses and adjectives associated with circuses.

ANSWERS

Thinking back
1 Mr Cosmo was coming to town.
2 A caravan appeared on the hill outside the town.
3 The horse was pulling the caravan.
4 A man, a woman, a boy and a girl appeared in the doorway of the caravan.

Thinking about it
1 Everyone in town was excited because Mr Cosmo was coming to town.
2 The people were surprised when they saw the caravan because no one was driving it.
3 Mr Cosmo was a conjuror. (The title tells you so.)
4 (open answer) The man, woman and children were probably Mr Cosmo, his wife and children.

Thinking it through
1 (open answer) Perhaps someone put them up during the night.
2 (open answer)
3 (open answer)
4 (open answer)

⇨ *Copymaster* Descriptions
Children are asked to match up six descriptions to six pictures of different children, by reading the clues carefully.

⇨ Descriptions

Name _____   Date _____

Cut out the descriptions and stick each one under the correct picture.

I have long hair.	I have curly hair.	I have a moustache.
I wear glasses.	I have a scar.	I wear a baseball cap.
I have a necklace.	I have two teeth missing.	My nose is crooked.

I have short hair.	My dress is spotted.	I wear a tee shirt.
I wear a tie.	I have dark glasses.	I have short, black hair.
I have freckles.	I have a bow in my hair.	I suck my thumb.

UNIT 17 Neigh, Cluck, Quack and Tweet — Introductory Book

FURTHER TEACHING OPPORTUNITIES

Text level

Reading comprehension
- Read the poem chorally. Have a different group of children read each verse.
- Discuss the layout of the poem (in verses, with four lines to each verse). Which lines rhyme?
- Look for the sound words in each verse.
- Find other animal poems to read.

Writing composition
- Write verses for other animals using the same structure and form.
- Notice the use of alliteration (lots of lovely food; quick, quack). Make up silly alliterative sentences, for example: 'The proud prince picked prize primroses.'

Sentence level

Grammatical awareness
- Read the text aloud with intonation and expression appropriate to the grammar and punctuation.

Sentence construction and punctuation
- The poem has a strong focus on verbs. Consider them as 'doing' words, for example: What does the horse do in verse 1? Write the answers as proper sentences, correctly punctuated.

Word level

Spelling
- Give the children common letter strings and search the poem to find words containing them, for instance, 'ack', 'ick', 'uck'.
- Select words from the poem and ask children to spell other words from them by analogy: for instance, tail – sail, pail, wail, mail.

Vocabulary extension
- Make a list of animal sound words.

ANSWERS

Thinking back
1. The speckled hen clucked.
2. The chirpy bird made a tweeting noise.
3. The chestnut horse neighed.
4. The yellow mother duck quacked.

Thinking about it
1. The parts of the horse's body mentioned are its mane, tail and hooves.
2. The hen has not got any chicks yet because its eggs have not yet hatched.
3. The word used for the duck's family is 'brood'.
4. The bird is singing in a tree.

Thinking it through
1. a) fly – high
   b) scratch – hatch
   c) brood – food
   d) tree – see
2. We say a horse gallops.
3. (open answer)
4. Moo sleepy brown cow,
   Moo at the gate.
   Will the farmer milk you
   _____(open answer)_____ ?

➡ *Copymaster* Animal Noises

Children are given ten animals and the ten noises associated with them. They have to match them up and write a sentence for each.

132

⇨ Animal Noises

Name _____   Date _____

Match up the animals and the noises they make.

A horse	grunts.	_____
A lamb	moos.	_____
A pig	neighs.	_A horse neighs._
A dog	clucks.	_____
A cow	bleats.	_____
A cat	quacks.	_____
A donkey	barks.	_____
A hen	hoots.	_____
A duck	purrs.	_____
An owl	brays.	_____

UNIT 18 Valley Farm

Introductory Book

FURTHER TEACHING OPPORTUNITIES

Text level

Reading comprehension
- Note the features of the poster – the use of a title and headings, an interesting illustrative picture, clear, concise bullet pointed notes (phrases not sentences).
- Discuss why clarity and brevity are important in posters in getting a message over quickly and clearly. How successful is the poster in achieving this?
- Discuss what other things you might like to have known which are not mentioned on the poster, such as a telephone number for queries, price of admission.

Writing composition
- Children might like to make an imaginary plan of the farm, putting in all the features mentioned.
- Make up a poster for a known local place of interest. Share ideas on what should go on it, how it should be laid out and so on.

Sentence level

Grammatical awareness
- Notice the use of adjectives. The function of these can be drawn attention to by asking 'what sort of' questions such as: 'What sort of farm machinery is in the museum?'

Sentence construction and punctuation
- No full stops are needed because only phrases are used on the poster. Note, however, the use of commas, separating the animals in the list.

Word level

Spelling
- The poster could be used as a springboard for work on many phonemes, such as 'ea', 'or', 'ar', 'oo'.
- Contrast the sound value of the 'ch' in chickens and machinery.
- Notice the same sound value of the 'or' in 'working' and 'er' in 'machinery'.

Vocabulary extension
- Brainstorm words connected with farming.
- What other sorts of museums are there? What is their purpose? What would you expect to find in them?

ANSWERS

1 False.
2 True.
3 True.
4 False.
5 True.

Thinking about it
1 You could eat your lunch in the lunchrooms.
2 You could buy something to eat at the café.
3 You could buy a present at the gift shop.
4 Valley Farm is easy to reach by car because it is near the motorway.
5 You could visit the farm on a school trip because schools are welcome.

Thinking it through
1 (open answer)
2 (open answer)
3 (open answer)

⇨ *Copymaster*
Looking for Information
Children are given pictures of a number of different reference books. They are then asked in which of the books they would find particular types of information.

➪ Looking for Information

Name _____ Date _____

a dictionary   a road atlas of Britain   a telephone directory
an atlas   a cookery book   a first aid book   a toy catalogue
the TV Times

Which book would I look in to find out:

▶ how to make a cake? _____

▶ the price of a toy I want? _____

▶ what a word means? _____

▶ where Italy is? _____

▶ how to bandage a cut? _____

▶ the time of my favourite programme? _____

▶ someone's telephone number? _____

▶ how to get to London? _____

Focus on Comprehension Teacher's Book 'A'. Text © Louis Fidge 1999
Illustrations © Nelson 1999. Published by Thomas Nelson and Sons Ltd 1999

Introductory Book / Copymaster / Unit 18

UNIT 19 Animal Homes

Introductory Book

FURTHER TEACHING OPPORTUNITIES

Text level

Reading comprehension
- Discuss what sort of text this is (information, non-fiction, factual).
- Draw attention to the fact that there is a paragraph about each animal. Discuss what a paragraph is. Note how key words are emboldened for emphasis.
- Discuss, too, how the illustration linked to each paragraph aids understanding.

Writing composition
- Research and write some similar notes, along similar lines, about other animals (such as squirrels or foxes).

Sentence level

Grammatical awareness
- Try re-reading the text but changing it into the singular, for example: 'A rabbit lives in a tunnel underground.' Point out what changes take place to ensure correct grammatical agreement.

Sentence construction and punctuation
- Ask children to make up questions for each other based on the text, and ensure they are punctuated correctly.

Word level

Spelling
- There are some interesting plural words that could be studied. Note how they change from the singular: words that just add 's' such as burrow; words in which the 'y' changes to 'ies' such as enemy; words in which the 'f' changes to 'v' such as leaf; unusual plurals such as 'foot' to 'feet'.

Vocabulary extension
- Do some work on opposites, based on words in the text, for example, safe, warm, light.
- Investigate and list other animal homes.

ANSWERS

Thinking back
1. Rabbits live in tunnels called <u>burrows</u>.
2. Moles have feet like <u>shovels</u>.
3. Moles use their feet to <u>dig</u>.
4. Hedgehogs eat <u>worms</u>.
5. Badgers live <u>underground</u>.

Thinking about it
1. Rabbits live underground to keep them safe from their enemies.
2. Moles are not seen very often because they spend most of their time underground.
3. Hedgehogs use piles of old leaves as a kind of nest.
4. Badgers are like moles because they live underground too.

Thinking it through
1. (open answer)
2. (open answer) Probably because they live most of their lives underground.
3. (open answer)

▶ *Copymaster* Animal Quiz
Children are given ten questions about ten different animals, and have to use their general knowledge to answer them. The names of the animals are given in a box.

➡ Animal Quiz

Name _____   Date _____

Choose an animal from the box to answer each question.

| horse | rabbit | bee | butterfly | frog |
| fox | owl | duck | hedgehog | squirrel |

Who am I?

I scamper and live in a burrow.   _____

I live in a hive and make honey.   _____

I live in a pond and croak.   _____

I hunt at night and have a sharp beak.   _____

I waddle and quack.   _____

I have hooves and live in a stable.   _____

I was once a caterpillar.   _____

I have a bushy tail and eat nuts.   _____

I have prickly spines and sleep in winter.   _____

I am like a brown dog and live in the woods.   _____

UNIT 20 Pooh Bear Gets Stuck

Introductory Book

FURTHER TEACHING OPPORTUNITIES

Text level

Reading comprehension
- What can be learnt about Pooh Bear from the extract?
- What can be gleaned about the relationships between the characters in the text?
- Have any of the children ever been in any situations where help had to be summoned?
- Have we ever blamed other things or people when we are in a difficult situation of our own making?
- Find and read other Pooh Bear stories. Contrast them and ask for children's opinions and preferences.
- Read some A A Milne poems about Christopher Robin.

Writing composition
- Write about how Christopher Robin might have extricated Pooh Bear.
- Make up some other stories in which Pooh Bear gets into trouble. Make them into a class anthology.

Sentence level

Grammatical awareness
- Read the text aloud, paying due care and attention to meaning and punctuation.

Sentence construction and punctuation
- Notice the use of speech marks in the story and the use of capital letters for people's names.

Word level

Spelling
- Start with the words 'hopeful' and 'careless' from the text and do some work on suffixing words with 'ful' (note only one 'l') and 'less'. Notice how antonyms can be made in this way, such as useful – useless. There are also several adverbs ending in 'ly' that could lead to work on suffixing.
- Read the word 'Christopher' and listen to the sound the 'ch' makes. Think of other words like this (chemist, echo, school).
- Look for words containing the phonemes 'aw' and 'ur'.

ANSWERS

Thinking back
1. True.
2. False.
3. True.
4. True.
5. False.

Thinking about it
1. Pooh Bear said it was because the front door was not big enough.
2. Rabbit said Pooh got stuck because he ate too much.
3. (open answer) Probably because Pooh was stuck too tightly.
4. The story says that Christopher Robin saw the front half of Pooh. Also, the picture shows that Pooh was coming out head first.

Thinking it through
1. a) (open answer)
   b) (open answer)
   c) (open answer)
2. You can tell Christopher Robin liked Pooh because it says in the text that he talked to Pooh in a loving voice.
3. (open answer)

⇨ *Copymaster* Us Two

This sheet contains a poem about Christopher Robin and Winnie the Pooh written by AA Milne. The sheet allows comparisons to be made between the unit in the book and the poem, contrasting texts with similar themes by the same author.

⇨ Us Two

Name _____ Date _____

Here is a rhyme written about Christopher Robin
and Pooh Bear by AA Milne.

Wherever I am, there's always Pooh,
There's always Pooh and Me.
Whatever I do, he wants to do,
"Where are you going today?" says Pooh:
"Well that's very odd 'cos I was too.
Let's go together," says Pooh, says he.
"Let's go together," says Pooh.

So wherever I am, there's always Pooh,
There's always Pooh and Me.
"What would I do?" I said to Pooh,
"If it wasn't for you," and Pooh said: "True,
It isn't much fun for One, but Two
Can stick together," says Pooh, says he.
"That's how it is," says Pooh.

1 How can you tell Christopher Robin and Pooh Bear are good friends?
   _____
   _____

2 Is this a poem or a story? How can you tell? _____
   _____

3 Who wrote it? _____

4 What does it have in common with Unit 20 in your book? _____
   _____

5 Which do you prefer, the story or the poem? Why? _____
   _____

UNIT 21 Our Family Comes From Around the World

Introductory Book

FURTHER TEACHING OPPORTUNITIES

Text level

Reading comprehension
- Try reading the poem in groups, with different groups taking responsibility for different lines or verses.
- After reading the poem, ask children to say what they liked (or disliked) about it.
- Discuss the theme of the poem. In what way can everyone be part of the same family? In what ways can everyone help make the world a better place?

Writing composition
- Use the poem as a stimulus for making a poem about the school 'family'.

Sentence level

Grammatical awareness
- It is important to take note of the punctuation in order to make sense of the poem. Some lines end with a comma, and therefore require a pause, whereas some lines do not, and should be run into the next line.

Word level

Spelling
- The rhyming words in the poem are a good way of demonstrating that not all words that sound alike are spelt in the same way.

Vocabulary extension
- The poem lends itself well to work on synonyms and antonyms.

ANSWERS

Thinking back
1. Our hair is straight. Our hair is curled.
2. We're girls. We're boys.
3. We're big. We're small.
4. We're young. We're old.
5. We laugh. We cry.

Thinking about it
Answers could include:
1. We have different hair styles.
2. We have different colour eyes.
3. We have different colour skins.
4. We are boys and girls.
5. We are big and small.
6. We are young and old.
7. We are short and tall.
8. We laugh and cry.
9. We work and play.

Thinking it through
1. (open answer)
2. We are all different in some ways. We all belong to one big family.
3. (open answer)
4. (open answer)

➡ *Copymaster* Odd One Out
This sheet involves classification. It involves looking at families or sets of objects and asks children to decide which item is the odd one out in each set. They then have to explain why.

⇨ Odd One Out

Name _____   Date _____

Underline the odd one out in each line.
Explain why it does not belong.

The <u>car</u> is the odd one out because <u>all the others are animals</u>.

The _____ is the odd one out because _____.

The _____ is the odd one out because _____.

The _____ is the odd one out because _____.

The _____ is the odd one out because _____.

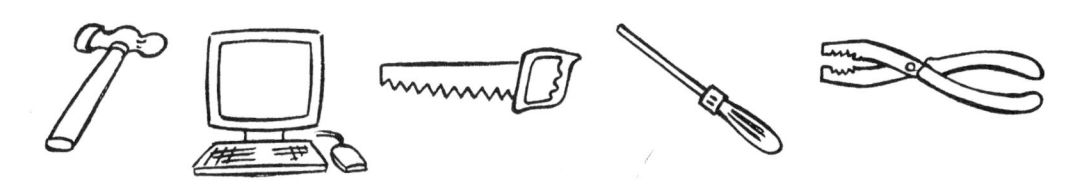

The _____ is the odd one out because _____.

UNIT 22 The Winter Hedgehog

Introductory Book

FURTHER TEACHING OPPORTUNITIES

Text level

Reading comprehension
- The hedgehog was puzzled about 'winter'. What things really puzzle the children?
- Was the hedgehog naughty or just curious and thoughtless?
- Discuss why the hedgehogs were collecting leaves, and what 'hibernate' means.

Writing composition
- The small hedgehog meets many other animals in his quest. Write about some he might see and what they say to him.
- The small hedgehog runs away and gets lost. Have any children ever been lost? Ask children to write about an adventure they have had.

Sentence level

Sentence construction and punctuation
- Ask children to write some questions about things that puzzle them.
- Do some research and find out more about hedgehogs. Write a fact file about them, based on simple sentences, such as Five Fascinating Facts about Hedgehogs.

Word level

Spelling
- Do some work on syllabification. Write the word 'afternoon' on the board and break it into syllables, by marking the syllable boundaries. Look for other multi-syllabic words in the text and do the same to them.
- Look for words ending with 'ing' and 'ed' in the text. Work out what the root word of each is.
- Look for examples of compound words, such as undergrowth, hedgehog, afternoon, overheard.

Vocabulary extension
- Write the months and seasons of the year in sequence.
- What words do children associate with each season? Brainstorm and list words and phrases.

ANSWERS

Thinking back
1. The hedgehogs gathered in a wood.
2. They were searching for leaves.
3. The smallest hedgehog went looking for winter.

Thinking about it
1. She described winter as very beautiful, but dangerous, cruel and very cold.
2. The small hedgehog couldn't sleep because he was excited and wanted to find out what winter was.
3. (open answer) He probably curled up and slept in some old leaves, or in a sheltered spot such as a hollow tree or an old rabbit burrow.
4. (open answer) Probably it was a cold, frosty winter morning.

Thinking it through
1. Children should provide at least 2 answers. Any of these are possible:
   determined   prickly   brave
   adventurous   foolish   curious
2. (open answer)
3. (open answer)

➡ *Copymaster* Hedgehogs

Children are given a brief passage about hedgehogs and asked to extract information from it, to be presented in the form of a grid.

➡ Hedgehogs

Name _____   Date _____

Hedgehogs are very common in Britain. They are found in a variety of habitats from woodlands to people's gardens. Hedgehogs grow up to 25 cm in length and weigh between 800-1400 grams. They are covered with prickly spines and roll up into a ball to protect themselves when attacked. Hedgehogs normally come out in the evenings and at night to look for food. They eat mainly small insects, worms and slugs. Hedgehogs sometimes live in old rabbit burrows or they make themselves nests of leaves for shelter. They usually have litters of 2-9 babies in the late spring.

Fill in the chart with some things you have learned.

	Facts about hedgehogs
Habitat	
Length	
Weight	
Appearance	
Diet	
Where they live	
Number of young	